Fanny Elssler in her dressing room at the Park Theatre, New York, 1840.

Oil painting by Thomas Sully after Henry Inman

IMAGES OF THE DANCE

Historical Treasures of the

Dance Collection 1581–1861

by Lillian Moore

The New York Public Library

Astor, Lenox and Tilden Foundations

New York

THE DANCING SCHOOLE.

1 *A seventeenth-century dancing school*

A book or a print that belongs to a great public library takes on a special vitality, almost a life of its own. Though it be of the greatest rarity and value, it is seldom permitted to languish very long under glass. It is used. Savored by active minds, scrutinized by eager eyes, it provides stimulation and inspiration; the polished product of the writer or painter is transmuted into the raw material of fresh creation.

The Dance Collection of the New York Public Library is a center for such magical activity. Fortunate in its subject, an art and pastime of the deepest cultural and social significance, it has expanded with spectacular rapidity. Since its inauguration by Dr Carleton Sprague Smith in 1944, it has grown from a small corner of the Music Division to the achievement of Division status on its own, probably the first such dance section in any public library. This extraordinary development would have been impossible without the tireless enthusiasm of its Curator, Genevieve Oswald, the generosity of its many donors, and the encouragement of the Library's farsighted Administration.

In the course of its growth, the Dance Collection has strengthened its resources to a phenomenal extent. The dance is a visual art, so its pictorial records are of primary importance. To an ever increasing degree, as the needs of its users have been clarified, it has acquired prints, photographs, and illustrated books on every conceivable aspect of its subject. In the course of building up a collection which would serve both the professional and the layman, the Division has amassed a store of treasures to delight the most fastidious connoisseur.

The period 1581–1861, covered in the present book, is rich in handsome delineations of the dance, in luxuriously illustrated books and fine prints. However, most of these highly desirable items are of the utmost scarcity. Originally issued in small quantities for a limited public,

they have been reduced by the vicissitudes of time until some survive just in single examples. With a policy of constructive acquisitiveness and the help of the dance world, the Dance Collection gradually built up archives of considerable importance. At the same time, individual collectors such as Lincoln Kirstein and Walter Toscanini (donor of the fabulous Cia Fornaroli Collection) through assiduous searching had formed valuable private collections. With the addition of these splendid donations, and the generosity of the Friends of the Dance Collection, the Division has become a real treasure-house of historical material.

A touchstone of the collection is its copy of John Playford's *The Dancing Master*, on whose title page the seventeenth-century dancing school appears. The first English dance book, it was published in no less than seventeen editions between 1651 and 1728, yet because it was a truly practical book, giving music and instructions for country dances, copies were literally worn out, until now they are rarer than emeralds. The Dance Collection's copy is handsomely boxed, but the little oblong book inside is shabby and fragile. Evidently it has furnished the patterns for many a merry measure—as it still can do.

2 Ballet Comique de la Reine

n Jonson was nine years old when the
llet Comique de la Reine was presented,
1581. He could scarcely have seen the
agnificent spectacle, given in Paris to
lebrate the betrothal of the Duc de
yeuse to Marguerite of Lorraine, sister
the Queen of France. Nevertheless he
ems to have owned the beautifully
inted account of it published by Ballard
the following year. His signature is
rawled on the title page of the Library's
py of the book, which is considered
e first actual ballet libretto. The *Ballet*
mique de la Reine undoubtedly
luenced the form of Jonson's masques,
oduced a quarter of a century later
the English court.

The same volume contains the
okplate of Horace Walpole, who
ssed seeing the Ballet Comique by two
nturies, but was such an assiduous
eatregoer that his famous *Letters* are
ppered with references to the
lebrated dancers of his time.

It was Catherine de' Medici who
troduced to France the Italian custom
elaborate banquet entertainments in
iich classic or allegorical legends were
d through entrées of dancing and
isic. Her director of court festivals, an
lian named Baltazarini da Belgiojoso
r Balthasar de Beaujoyeux), was
sponsible for the staging and
oreography of the *Ballet Comique de la*
ine. Presented at the Petit Bourbon on
ctober 15, 1581, it told the story of
rce. The lavish spectacle was enacted
professional artists and the ladies and
ntlemen of the Court, including the
ueen herself. It lasted from ten at night
til five o'clock in the morning.

The eighteen engravings in the libretto
e attributed to J. Patin, painter to the
ng. The first depicts the opening
ene, with an actor (the Sieur de la
oche) delivering the prologue; another
ows the entrée of the four virtues of
ith, Justice, Charity, and Prudence,
earing elaborate star-studded costumes
d carrying symbolic emblems.

Towards the end of the sixteenth centu
there was very little technical differenc
between the social dances of the
aristocracy and the dancing seen in th
entrées of the court ballets. The latter
had more complicated floor patterns an
more formal groupings, as well as mor
elaborate costuming. Nevertheless the
steps and positions of ballroom dances
were almost identical with those used i
the ballets.

The handsome dance manuals
published at this period consequently
reveal much about the background of t
theatrical dance, although they describ
the pavanes and galliards popular at th
time, and the illustrations depict courtie
dancing for their own amusement.
Fabritio Caroso's *Il Ballarino* originall
appeared in Venice in 1581. It is this fi
edition which has furnished the engravi
of two dancers, whose dignity and
elegance are so typical of that era.

Cesare Negri, working in Milan, was
strongly influenced by the Spaniards w
then occupied the city. His *Spagnolett*
is a galliard, lively and gay; some of th
steps and figures, as well as the positic
of the four dancers shown here, bear a
strong resemblance to those still used i
square dances. England's first Queen
Elizabeth loved galliards, and the
spagnoletta was a favorite at her court.
The Dance Collection's superb copy o
Negri's *Le Gratie d'Amore* is notable fo
its sumptuous binding (royal blue
morocco exquisitely tooled in gilt),
which helps to make it one of the mos
extravagantly beautiful books imaginab

While Caroso and Negri were
compiling their invaluable manuals at
the Italian courts, their contemporary
Marten de Vos was painting in Antwe
His lusty scene, engraved by Joannes
Galle, depicts a village festival and a
more robust kind of dance: a strappin
peasant boisterously shows off his
agility as he trips over and around a
cluster of eggs, presumably without
breaking one.

4 *Dancers from Caroso's* Il Ballarino   5 *Cesare Negri's dance* Lo Spagnoletto

Egg dance

When Ferdinand II, grand duke of
Tuscany, married Vittoria della Rovere,
princess of Urbino, in 1637, the city of
Florence was the scene of fabulous
festivities which included a magnificent
equestrian pageant, or "horse ballet,"
and a musical drama, *Le Nozze degli Dei*,
which was a precursor of both opera and
ballet as we know them today.

The equestrian ballet was based on the
theme of *Jerusalem Liberated*, and it
featured very complicated choreographic
manoeuvres arranged by Agniolo Ricci
and executed by highly trained horses
and their equally skillful riders. Ricci
was an expert in the staging of such
spectacles; he had created them for the
dukes of Tuscany as early as 1615, when
he was responsible for the *Guerra d'Amore*,
given under the patronage of the Medici.
For his graceful four-footed dancers
Ricci devised evolutions as intricate and
precise as those now performed by the
Rockettes at Radio City Music Hall.
Dancing horses were once cultivated in
most of the great courts of Europe; today
they survive only in the glorious white
Lippizan stallions of Vienna, whose
thrilling performances are a living
reminder of the splendid horse ballets
of the baroque period.

The artist who immortalized Ricci's
equine choreography was Stefano della
Bella, a Florentine etcher and engraver
who was strongly influenced by Jacques
Callot. He is responsible also for the very
striking scene from the Ballet of the Sea
in *Le Nozze degli Dei*. Designed by
Alfonso Parigi and staged by the same
choreographer, Angiolo Ricci, who
directed the horse ballet, it represented a
celebration in honor of Neptune and
Amphitrite, who are seen seated in raised
thrones at the rear of the stage, while
Imeneo, cloud-borne, hovers in the sky
at the left. In the foreground are thirteen
dancers representing tritons, or sea gods.
Three of them, lightly supported by two
others, are executing steps that look
exactly like modern *entrechats*, while two

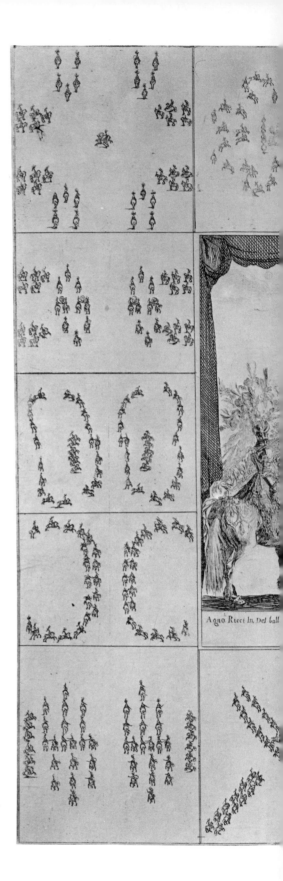

Agno Ricci In Del ball

7 *An equestrian ballet in Florence*

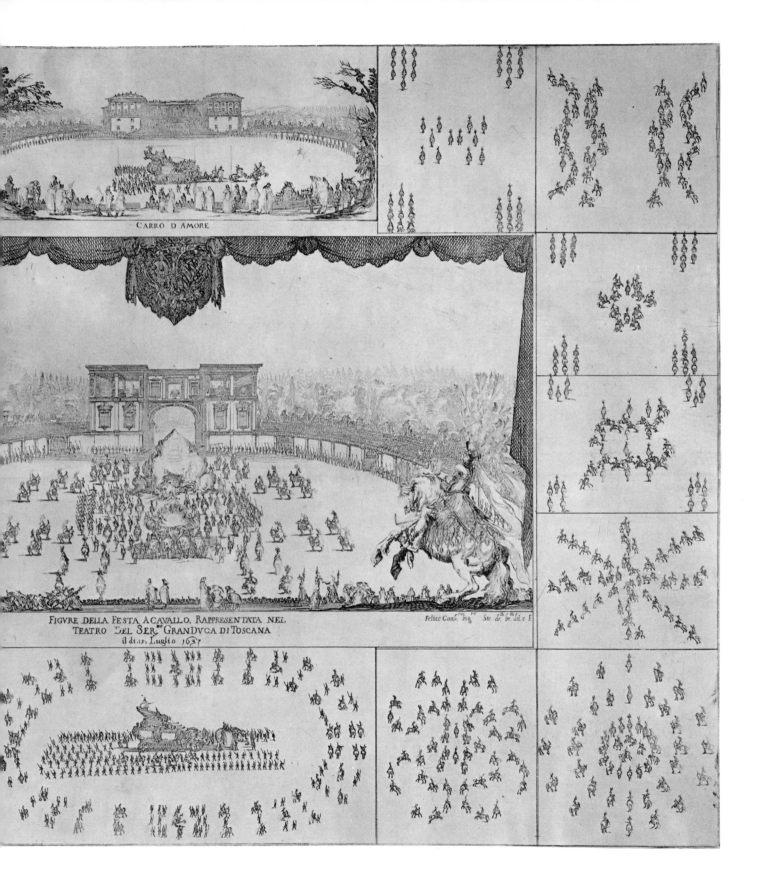

CARRO D'AMORE

FIGVRE DELLA FESTA A CAVALLO, RAPPRESENTATA NEL
TEATRO DEL SER.ᵐᵒ GRANDVCA DI TOSCANA
il dì 15. Luglio 1637

Felice Gonſ. Ing.ᵉ   Sté. de⁸ Bⁱˡ. del. e Fᵉ.

8 *Scene from* Le Nozze degli Dei

re are vaulting over the backs of sea
ses. Although many nobles
ticipated in this performance, the
cers must have been professionals
ned in acrobatics and the elements of
at was beginning to emerge as classic
et technique.

n France, the patronage of Louis XIV,
ardent dancer in his youth and an
ightened benefactor of the arts
oughout his long life, had brought
ut the establishment of the Académie
yale de Danse in 1661 and the
adémie Royale de Musique eight years
r. These two organizations soon
mbined with the school for training
fessional dancers which Louis
nded in 1672 to form the Paris Opéra,
ich has remained a center of ballet
duction and technical instruction for
rly three centuries.

n Lulli's opera-ballet *Le Triomphe de
mour*, in 1681, female professional
cers first appeared on the French
ge. Mlle Lafontaine, the *première
seuse*, was immediately acclaimed as
e queen of the dance." Among the
er participants were Charles-Louis
uchamp, first choreographer of the
éra, and Louis Pécourt, who was to
cceed him. The theme of the ballet
cerned the homage of gods and
ddesses, nymphs, pleasures, and
ious peoples of the world to the
powerful god of love.

ean Berain, official designer of the
éra, created the settings and costumes
Le Triomphe de l'Amour. One of the
st effective was that of an Indian, a
ower of Bacchus. Berain's son, also
led Jean, designed the sculptor's
tume for an unidentified production,
ut 1700. Artists of the time frequently
cumbered their costumes with assorted
ects associated with the profession of
character depicted. A cook, for
mple, might be loaded down with
ts, pans, and even vegetables. Here,
sculptor's chisel is conspicuous.
ean Berain the elder was the designer

9 *Costume for* Le Triomphe de l'Amour   10 *Costume of a sculptor*   13

of *Les Fêtes de l'Amour et de Bacchus*, first given in Paris in 1672, and repeated at Versailles two years later. This "comedy in music" actually consisted of interludes and divertissements from several of the comedy-ballets of Molière, cleverly adapted by the composer Jean-Baptiste Lulli, so that they made one cohesive whole. The pastorale from *Le Bourgeois Gentilhomme* provided the greater part of the *Fêtes de l'Amour*, but the work also included sections of *George Dandin, Les Amants Magnifiques*, and *La Pastorale Comique*. Charles-Louis Beauchamp not only directed the ballets, but danced in them, while the librettist Philippe Quinault, who had collaborated with Lulli on the arrangement of the production, was responsible for its staging. The machines were constructed by the brilliant Italian theatrical architect Carlo Vigarani.

In Jean LePautre's exquisitely detailed engraving of *Les Fêtes de l'Amour et de Bacchus* it is possible to see not only the dancers on the stage and the musicians suspended and half-hidden in the trees, but the entire proscenium of the theatre at Versailles, and even the faces of some of the spectators, as well as the majestic backs of the royal party.

Lulli has been accused of taking advantage of the ailing Molière (who died in 1673) in appropriating his work and incorporating it in *Les Fêtes de l'Amour et de Bacchus*. A libretto published in 1672 did not even mention the dramatist, although his lines made up most of the text. At any rate, the lavish production consolidated Lulli's power over the newly organized Paris Opéra. *Les Fêtes de l'Amour et de Bacchus* became so popular that it was revived at intervals until 1738.

By 1700, an effective system of dance notation had been formulated and published. The author of *Choregraphie, ou l'Art de décrire la Dance* was Raoul Ager Feuillet, a dancing master who had lived in obscurity until his great work was completed. Many authorities contend

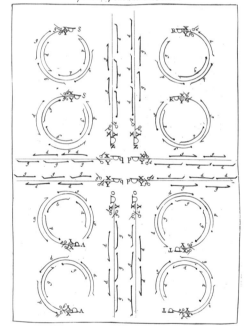

that the true creator of dance notation was the distinguished choreographer Beauchamp, who is said to have protested the publication of Feuillet's book on the grounds that it was based on his own ideas and theories. Indeed, P. Siris, who translated *Choregraphie* into English in 1706, commented that Beauchamp had taught him its principles more than eighteen years earlier. Nevertheless, not a scrap of dance notation by Beauchamp has ever been found, and if he did actually conceive the plan for the Feuillet system he apparently preserved no written evidence of his invention.

The Feuillet choreography is decorative as well as practical, and its diagrams often have a rhythmic airy grace. The one reproduced here is notable for its spare and classic symmetry. Equally intriguing are the designs for the dance *Le Rigaudon de la Paix*, which furnish the motifs for the cover paper of this book.

Feuillet dedicated his *Choregraphie* to the ballet master Louis Pecour, many of whose dances he transcribed and published. Apparently the Feuillet system was widely used during his lifetime, for he published collections of dances, some of which had been performed by such celebrated artists as the Paris Opéra stars Jean Ballon and Marie-Thérèse Subligny, at intervals over a period of fifteen years. In England, E. Pemberton and John Weaver were prompt to publish translations of Feuillet's work.

Quite early in the eighteenth century it was introduced in Germany as well, for Gottfried Taubert devoted an impressive section of his *Rechtschaffener Tantzmeister*, one of the first German treatises on the dance, to an exposition of Feuillet's notation. In the charming frontispiece to his book, Taubert reveals his two primary interests—books and ballet—by placing his seven dancers in a library, with a backdrop of crowded bookshelves, while his "conscientious dancing master"

meditates on the theory and practice of his art. Taubert, born about 1680, was teacher in Danzig and in Leipzig, whe the *Rechtschaffener Tantzmeister* was published in 1717.

Eight years later Pierre Rameau's *L Maître à Danser* appeared in Paris. Its illustrations were drawn and engraved the author, who was a dancing master rather than a graphic artist by professic so they are crude in execution but unusually authoritative insofar as the dance poses are concerned. In *Le Maîtr Danser* the five positions of the feet, fir definitively established by Beauchamp and still the essential base of all classic dancing, are carefully delineated. Exce for the fact that in Rameau's time the turned-out position of feet and legs wa not so extreme as it is today, his figure might still serve as admirable models. Rameau analyzes the steps used in the ballets and social dances of his time, many of which have survived in somewl altered form but under the same name (*jetés*, *chassés*, *entrechats*, *pirouettes*, etc) He also describes the exact conduct of formal court ball under Louis XV, wit the dances following a prescribed orde first the branle, then the gavotte, and finally the most popular dance of the century, the minuet. The king was alwa the first to dance it. After he had resum his place on the throne at the end of t ballroom, the prince next in rank led forward the lady of his choice. It is the charming formality of this moment, at the commencement of the second minu that Rameau has illustrated in the plat reproduced here.

The books of Feuillet and Rameau, l those of Caroso and Negri, are cornerstones of the Dance Collection. Both of those represented here came from the Lincoln Kirstein Collection, and have a special interest because the were the copies he used in writing his *Dance: A Short History of Classical Theatrical Dancing*, published in 1935

14 *Minuet from Rameau's* Maître à Danser

15 *Marie Camargo*

[R]ameau's contemporary, Marie Camargo, [m]ade her debut at the Paris Opéra in [17]26. She received much of her early [tr]aining from a man, David Dumoulin, [w]ho taught her steps such as the *entrechat* [an]d *cabriole* which no woman had [pr]eviously mastered. Thus she became [th]e first ballerina to achieve brilliance [an]d virtuosity as well as grace. Proud of [th]e speed and precision of her flashing [fe]et, Camargo daringly shortened her [sk]irts to the middle of the calf. The [he]ight of her jumps obliged her to adopt [th]e *caleçon de precaution* ("precautionary [dr]awers") considered unnecessary by [th]e dignified *danseuses* who had preceded [he]r. Camargo is also credited with the [in]vention of the heel-less ballet slipper, [alt]hough contemporary pictures [in]variably show her wearing tiny heels, [lik]e the other dancers of her time.

Praised by Voltaire, Camargo was a [fav]orite subject of the painter Nicholas [La]ncret. One of his portraits of her hangs [in] the National Gallery in Washington, [D.]C.; another, on which the Dance [Co]llection's fine engraving by Laurent [Ca]rs is based, is in the Wallace [Co]llection, London.

The basic costume of the male classic [da]ncer, at that time, was the *tonnelet* or [sh]ort, full skirt, very similar in shape [to] the *tutu* adopted by ballerinas more [th]an a century later and still very much [in] favor. Plumes, ribbons, tassels, [ga]rlands, and rosettes were used [in]discriminately to trim everything from [th]e crisply stylized costume of the [da]nseur noble who played Zephyre, [sh]own here in the engraving by Jean [Ba]ptiste Martin, to the less formal but [alm]ost equally ornate one worn by a [ch]aracter dancer in the role of a Spanish [pe]asant. It was against such sumptuous [bu]t highly improbable theatrical dress [th]at Jean Georges Noverre made his [elo]quent plea for the reform of ballet [cos]tume in his epoch-making treatise, *[Let]tres sur la Danse et sur les Ballets*, [1]760.

16 *Costume for Zephyre* 17 *Spanish peasant costume in a ballet* 19

In the ballrooms of the eighteenth
century, the minuet reigned supreme. I
elegance, dignity, and mannered grace
reflected the atmosphere of the French
court, but it was equally popular in les
aristocratic surroundings, and althoug|
George Bickham's *An Easy Introduction
to Dancing, or, The Movements in the
Minuet Fully Explained* is now a rarity.
it once sold for a shilling and served as
simple "teach yourself to dance" manu
Bickham was an English engraver with
fairly extensive knowledge of several ar
He is remembered for his work on
calligraphy, *The Universal Penman*, an
the attractive plates of his two folio
volumes, *The Musical Entertainer*.

Originally a lively rustic dance of th
French province of Poitou, the minuet
was danced in three-four time, and
derived its name from its small, dainty
steps (*menus pas*). It was a favorite of
composer Lulli, who first incorporated
it in the musical suite; it is found in wo
of Handel and Bach, Haydn and Moza
and Beethoven transformed it into the
symphonic scherzo. The dance likewis
went through many changes, while
retaining its essential character.

The stately promenade of the minu
punctuated by formal poses and preci
pointings of the feet, made it almost a
ritual, in which the presentation of a
hand was a carefully studied and
supremely gracious gesture. The high
priests of the ceremony were the danc
masters, arbiters of style and sometim
—like the celebrated Marcel, who mac
even his royal pupils submit to his
strictures—absolute dictators. Marcel |
been a first dancer at the Paris Opéra
François Nivelon came from the more
democratic theatrical background of t
Paris fairs, Lincoln's Inn Fields, and
Drury Lane. Nevertheless he was an
expert on the elaborate etiquette of th
minuet, and he presents it with
unquestionable authority in his
handsome book, *The Rudiments of
Genteel Behavior*.

18 *A minuet, from Bickham's treatise, 1738*

Lady in a minuet   20   *Gentleman in a minuet*   21

The age of the minuet was also the heyday of Hogarth and other similarly caustic satirists of the social scene. It was John Collet, a prominent member of this distinctive English school, who painted *Grown Gentlemen Taught to Dance*, a devastating comment on the hopeless (but well remunerated) efforts of a dancing master to transform a clumsy oaf into an ornament of the ballroom, while another unfortunate student tries to force his feet and knees into the accepted turned-out position while he waits for his own lesson. The picture on the wall depicts the ideal to be emulated— "Madame Elastique," the personification of charm and facility.

There is little doubt that "Madame Elastique" was the dazzling star of the King's Theatre, Covent Garden, and Drury Lane, Anne Auretti, whose engraved portrait by Gérard Scotin is one of the most desirable and elusive souvenirs of eighteenth-century ballet in England. Horace Walpole was among Mlle Auretti's admirers. In a letter to Horace Mann, late in 1742, he mentioned the opera parties which he and Lord Holderness had been organizing for the performances of Auretti and La Barberina. Although Barberina was Italian and Auretti French (she came from Provence), they belonged to the same school of dancing, the vigorous and exciting one inaugurated by Camargo. Barberina, like Marie Camargo, was noted for her *entrechats*; Auretti excelled in the *pirouette* and the *gargouillade* (a complicated aerial manoeuvre which involves twirling the right foot in one direction while the left goes the opposite way). She was noted for her spirited character work, including Dutch and Polish numbers and even a "Savage Dance" in her extensive repertoire.

During most of her seasons in London, where she retained her popularity for more than twenty years, Anne Auretti was accompanied by a sister (or daughter?) named Janeton, who was

23   *A dance in Otaheite, 1777*

almost equally attractive. The Aurettis danced together in the company of David Garrick, known for his taste and discrimination in matters concerning the ballet. His wife, the former Mlle Violette, had been a ballerina before her marriage to the great actor.

It was no accident that audiences in eighteenth-century London were intrigued by Mlle Auretti's "Savage Dance." *Robinson Crusoe*, published in 1719, had been a best seller, arousing considerable curiosity about tropical islands and their exotic inhabitants. This was a period of exploration and discovery, especially in the Pacific Ocean, where the long voyages of the Frenchman Bougainville and the English sea captains Gilbert, Byron, and Cook put innumerable remote and glamorous islands on the map.

When Captain James Cook embarked on his third and final expedition to the south seas, in 1776, he took with him a young artist named John Webber, an Englishman of Swiss descent, who had studied painting in Bern and Paris, and for a single year attended the Royal Academy, London. He was only twenty-six at the commencement of the fatal voyage, which ended in disaster when Cook was murdered by natives on the beach at Kona, Hawaii, in 1779. Webber witnessed the event, and made it the subject of his most famous picture.

Before the tragedy, however, the expedition had visited many other islands of the Pacific. It was at Tahiti (then known as Otaheite), in 1777, that Webber recorded the seductive dance which had been presented in Cook's honor, on the command of the native chief, Otoo. Tahiti had been discovered by Bougainville in 1767, and evidences of European influence were already discernible in the elaborate costumes worn by the dancers, although their rippling arms and swaying hips betray the fact that Polynesian dances at that period bore a recognizable relationship to those still preserved today.

Cook's visit to Tahiti was the subject of a ballet as early as 1789, when Antonio Muzzarelli's *Il Capitano Cook all'Isola degli Ottaiti* was produced at the Teatro alla Scala, Milan, with Pietro Angiolini in the cast. More popular, however, was the "grand serious pantomime" *The Death of Captain Cook*, first given at the Théâtre de l'Ambigu Comique, Paris, in 1788, and reproduced with enormous success at Covent Garden, London, early in the following year. *The Death of Captain Cook* reached American shores in 1793, when the Old American Company presented it at the John Street Theatre, New York. A superior production, insofar as the dancing was concerned, was undoubtedly that given in Charleston a year later, when the cast included Jean Baptiste Francisquy, Alexander Placide, Mme Placide, and Master Louis Duport.

Another navigator who caught the imagination of dramatists and choreographers was the Comte Jean François de La Pérouse, whose mysterious disappearance in the course of a voyage around the world in 1788 was later discovered to have been caused by a shipwreck on the reefs at Vanikoro, in the Santa Cruz group of the Solomon Islands. His adventures were the theme of a pantomime produced in London in 1801, and later reproduced all over Europe and America.

Webber's print of *A Dance in Otaheite* has contributed to the creation of a ballet in comparatively recent years. The Dance Collection's copy formerly belonged to Lincoln Kirstein, who commissioned Eugene Loring's ballet *Yankee Clipper* in 1937 for the American Ballet Caravan, of which he was director. Although the costumes were designed by Charles Rain, that worn by the ballerina Marie Jeanne in the Tahitian sequence was directly inspired by Webber's engraving.

While hardy explorers were boldly enlarging the horizons of civilization, Louis XV and his current favorite, Mme de Pompadour, reigned over a court where the most prodigal extravagance was merely the order of the day. During the carnival season of 1763, Versailles was the scene of a whole series of balls enlivened by elaborate and carefully rehearsed entertainments. The climax of one such fête, that of February 8, has been delineated in an engraving by F. N. Martinet after M. A. Slodtz. Given on the orders of the Duc de Duras, first gentleman of the King's chamber, the ball was directed by Papillon de la Ferté, who in his capacity as comptroller of the *menus-plaisirs du Roi* exerted considerable power over the affairs of the Paris Opéra as well as those of the court.

In his journal, M de la Ferté described this as one of the most lavish balls of the winter. The ballroom was decorated with festoons of flowers held in place by clusters of diamonds, while the chandeliers were suspended by floral garlands interwoven with jewels. Two ballets were performed, but no professional dancers appeared; the participants were the noblest ladies and gentlemen of the court. *Les Élémens*, which included entrées for Earth, Air, Fire, and Water, was so much admired that it had to be repeated. So did *La Noce du Village*, in which the Prince de Condé danced the role of the bridegroom and the Marquise de Duras that of the bride. The Duc d'Orléans played the lord of the village, the Duchesse de Mazarin his lady. The charming maypole dance depicted in the engraving was probably part of the wedding celebration.

Among the pampered courtiers at Versailles, Papillon de la Ferté probably encountered no one so difficult to handle as the temperamental Gaetan Vestris, undisputed star of the Opéra and the greatest dancer of the day. His preposterous vanity led Vestris to declare that the century had produced only

24 *May Ball at Versailles*

JASON ET MEDEE   BALLET TRAGIQUE.

25   Jason et Medée (*Baccelli, Vestris, Simonet*)

ee great men: Frederick the Great,
ltaire, and himself. His arrogance was
tched only by the brilliance of his art.
e lightness, precision, and harmonious
bility of his dancing were unsurpassed.
superb performer, he had an instinctive
ent for acting which enabled him to
cel in the dramatic ballets of Noverre.
Medée et Jason, created in Stuttgart in
63, was one of the most impressive
rks of the great reformer, who believed
t ballet should be expressive, not
rely entertaining. Vestris danced in
e première, supervised its first Paris
oduction in 1770, and in 1781 had the
dacity to present it in London as his
n work.

Gaetan's twenty-one-year-old son
uguste, the fruit of his liaison with the
lerina Marie Allard, shared the
tastic success of that London season.
uguste was gifted with a phenomenal
ility to leap and turn, an endowment
ich Gaetan modestly attributed to the
t that Auguste had the advantage of
mself as father! The furore caused by
e two Vestris was so great that before
uguste's benefit performance, when
ey appeared together, the House of
mmons adjourned so that all its
embers might attend. That night's
ceipts were fourteen hundred pounds,
cording to Horace Walpole, who was
used that he could see the Vestris
nce and still remain in his senses.

In the London production of *Medée et*
son, Adelaide Simonet danced Medea,
etan Vestris played her faithless lover,
d the bewitching Giovanna Baccelli
s Creusa, the innocent victim of her
venge. The electrifying climax of the
llet, when the enraged Medea confronts
e lovers, has been depicted by John
ydell in a stunning engraving, a jewel
the Cia Fornaroli Collection. In spite
the artificiality of their costumes and
iffures, the emotions of the protagonists
rly burn through the paper, and it is
sy to understand why Noverre's ballets
re so revolutionary and so moving.

Giovanna Baccelli was one of the mos[t]
fascinating personalities who ever gra[ced]
the London stage. A sensitive artist w[ho]
could arouse an audience to pity and
sympathy in a tragic role like Creusa,
she was equally enchanting in the
sparkling comedy of Maximilien Gard[el's]
Ninette à la Cour and the classic measu[re]
of a *chaconne* or a *loure*. Her beauty
captivated the Duke of Dorset, who
installed her in luxury at his magnific[ent]
ancestral home, Knole, and had her
painted by Gainsborough and Sir Jos[hua]
Reynolds. The Dance Collection's
superb mezzotint by John Jones
reproduces Gainsborough's full-lengt[h]
portrait.

The vivacious *pas de trois* which
inspired the lively etching by Pierre L[?]
was danced by three of the most popu[lar]
performers of pre-Revolutionary Fran[ce.]
Marie Madeleine Guimard had a piqua[nt]
delicacy and radiant charm which
enhanced every role she undertook.
Passionately devoted to her art, she m[ade]
it one of the glories of the Paris Opér[a.]
Off stage, however, she was capricious
and wilful, and since her protectors
included several of the most influentia[l]
men in France, her power was extensi[ve.]
More than once she led her fellow danc[ers]
in revolt against the dictatorial direct[or]
of the Opéra.

Guimard's favorite partner was Jea[n]
Dauberval, remembered now as the
choreographer of *La Fille mal Gardée*,[a]
ballet so soundly constructed that it h[as]
survived in outline for nearly two
centuries, although its original steps ha[ve]
been lost. Dauberval had imagination,
wit, and intelligence. In his choreograp[hy]
he knew how to blend dancing and acti[ng]
imperceptibly, so that the story flowed
naturally through the movement. A
performer of enormous vitality and
versatility, he relished comedy roles as
much as classic *pas*. He was well paire[d]
with Guimard and Marie Allard, whos[e]
outstanding characteristic was her
spontaneous, joyous delight in dancing[.]

Marie Madeleine Guimard, Jean Dauberval, and Marie Allard

With the French Revolution, most of favorites of the old regime vanished i exile or retirement. New stars arose t replace them, and by 1806 even the jur Vestris, Auguste, was menaced by a younger rival, the sensational dancer Louis Antoine Duport. In that year J Berchoux published *La Danse, ou Les Dieux de l'Opéra*, a satirical epic poem celebrating the bitter struggle between them. The striking frontispiece depict the defeat of the forty-six-year-old veteran, who has fallen before Duport faultless *écarté*. Two years later, Dupo relinquished his still contested positio in Paris to go to Russia, where his triumphs were recorded by Tolstoy in *War and Peace*. Because his professio journey was also an elopement, and h companion the celebrated actress Mlle George, mistress of Napoleon, Duport was obliged to flee France in the midd of the night, disguised as a woman. H never danced in Paris again. Escaping from Russia just before Napoleon's invasion, he became a favorite in Naples. Eventually, as manager of the Vienna Opera, he discovered the tiny pupil who blossomed into the incomparable Fanny Elssler.

In London the principal home of ba at this time was the splendid King's Theatre in the Haymarket, the subjec of an exquisite aquatint by Bluck after Thomas Rowlandson. It clearly shows distinctive curving apron of the stage, approved by some dancers but heartil disliked by Elssler, who, when she appeared there in the 1830s, felt that half the audience was behind her.

Ballerina at the King's Theatre fror 1796 to 1807 was Mlle Parisot, whose debut created quite a stir because she was exceptionally limber, and did not hesitate to raise her legs far higher, in arabesques and other classic poses, th was customary at the time. Critics call her an "attitudinarian" rather than a dancer, but she was actually extendin the boundaries of ballet technique.

32   *Scene from a ballet by Viganò, 1812*

wo artists who survived the vicissitudes
the Revolution and the Empire to serve
e Paris Opéra after the restoration of
e Bourbons were Pierre and Marie
rdel. A contemporary of Auguste
estris, Pierre Gardel turned to
oreography early in his career,
hough he continued to dance and play
me parts for many years. One of his
st popular ballets was *Psyché*, created
his wife in 1790, when she was still
le Miller. Jean Prud'hon's delicate
pple engraving shows her in this, her
orite role, which she danced until her
irement in 1816.

A choreographer of far greater
nsequence was Salvatore Viganò, an
lian pupil of Jean Dauberval, who
veloped his theories and those of his
eceptor, Noverre, into a form of ballet
ich was powerfully dramatic. After
ing his *Mirra*, Stendhal compared
ganò to Shakespeare, declaring him a
nius of equal stature. Beethoven's only
let, *Prometheus*, was composed for
ganò.

One of his most remarkable
laborators was Alessandro Sanquirico,
o designed the scenery for most of the
numental works Viganò produced at
e Teatro alla Scala, Milan, from 1811
til his death ten years later. Sanquirico
ll understood the heroic and primitive
emes which inspired the great
oreographer, and translated them onto
vas with a sweeping simplicity. One
the first settings Sanquirico provided
Viganò was that of *L'Alunno della*
umenta, ossia Ippotoo Vendicato, in 1812.
The late Cia Fornaroli and her
sband, Walter Toscanini, ardent
ievers in the principles advocated by
ganò, assiduously collected materials
ncerning the work of their great
mpatriot. The handsome Sanquirico
atint comes from their Viganò
hives, which have enriched the Dance
llection to an immeasurable extent,
d have, through microfilms, been
seminated to many other libraries.

33 *Pierre Gardel*   34 *Marie Gardel*

During the Empire, the quadrille had
supplanted the minuet as the most
favored of ballroom dances. Since the
days of Caroso and Negri there had be
social dances in which couples advance
and retreated, turned their partners an
circled around each other. The quadri
of the early nineteenth century was
danced in a square formation. It had f
set figures: the *Chaîne Anglaise* (later
called *le Pantalon*), *L'Eté, la Poule, la
Pastourelle*, and *la Finale*. The steps
were complicated ones, borrowed from
the classical ballet. A pattern of *chassé
and *assemblés* called the *pas d'été* gave i
name to the second figure, glimpsed he
in Lebas's graceful engraving of four
couples in a quadrille.

Other steps demanded in a properly
executed quadrille were the *jeté, balan
coupé*, and *changement de pied*, while ar
expert would occasionally show off his
dexterity with a neatly crossed
entrechat-quatre. Such intricacies requir
instruction and practice. The dancing
school not only prospered; it subjecte
its aristocratic pupils to the same
artificial instruments of torture employ
at that time by professional dancers: t
grooved box which forcibly wrenched
the feet into a turned-out position, an
the frame of hinged boards which did
same for the knees and thighs. This
device is shown at the left of the delicat
satirical drawing of an *académie de dar
by an anonymous but keenly observan
artist. As he instructs a lightly clad
young lady, the dancing master, his
powerfully developed calf muscles
bulging, scrapes away at his tiny *poche
Until piano accompaniment was adop
late in the century, this little pocket
violin was the indispensable aid of all
dancing teachers.

The most celebrated of ballet
pedagogues, Carlo Blasis, formulated l
theories before he was twenty-five. Hi
*Traîté Elémentaire, théorique et pratiqu
de la Danse*, published in 1820, is one
the keystones of dance literature. In i

35   *A French dancing school*

36   *Four couples dancing a quadrille*

clarified the fundamental principles
classical theatrical dancing, and
ablished the positions which are still
e basis of ballet training today.
Born in Naples in 1795, Blasis in his
uth danced in Marseilles, Lyon,
rdeaux, and other cities of France.
ter a brief term in Paris he went to
lan, where he worked directly under
lvatore Viganò. A man of broad general
lture, Blasis wrote extensively on such
ried subjects as music, drama, and
story. An avid student of painting and
ulpture, he was also well versed in the
erature of several nations, and
oroughly grounded in musical
mposition. In spite of the range of his
owledge, he seems to have lacked the
eative imagination which makes a great
oreographer. Although he produced
llets for nearly half a century, from
19, when he choreographed *Il Finto*
udatorio at La Scala, Milan, until 1864,
en he staged several works in Moscow,
was as a teacher and theoretician that
asis won enduring fame.
In 1837, following a severe leg injury,
asis and his wife Annunciata Ramaccini
cepted the directorship of the ballet
ademy at La Scala. There they trained
ch stars of the romantic ballet as
malia Ferraris, Flora Fabbri, Sofia
oco, Giovanna Ciocca, and Marietta
derna. Established luminaries,
cluding Fanny Cerrito, Carlotta Grisi,
rolina Rosati, and the American
llerina Augusta Maywood, profited
m his lessons whenever their
ofessional engagements brought them
Milan.
His comprehensive artistic education
d given Blasis practical training in the
aphic arts, and he himself was
sponsible for the little drawings which
ustrate his *Traîté Elémentaire*. Notable
their clear-cut simplicity, they are
finitive representations of the classic
llet positions. Those illustrated here
ow an extension in the second position
th the leg at hip level (as it is used in

38 *Classical poses from Theleur's* Letters on Dancing

the *pirouette à la seconde*, for example)
and three variations of the *effacé*, with
the arms used in different ways.

In 1831, in London, an obscure and
rather mysterious dancing teacher named
Theleur (possibly a Frenchification of
plain Taylor) published an attractive
little book called *Letters on Dancing*.
Some of its illustrations proclaim him as
a follower of Blasis, for they consist of
separate poses from the Italian master's
Traîté arranged in novel combinations.

Such a group is one based on the
variations of the *effacé* as drawn by Blasis.
Theleur has put them together to form
a decorative little theatrical composition,
embellished, in the typical taste of the
time, with scarves and garlands.

Theleur was a curious and rather
pathetic individual. After the appearance
of his book he began to fancy himself a
great dancer as well as a theoretician.
Although he was about fifty, he turned up
at the Paris Opéra and applied for the
position of *premier danseur*. Not
surprisingly, he was turned down.
However, the hardened professionals of
the Opéra were not above a little fun at
his expense. He had been given the
freedom of the theatre, perhaps in
recognition of his position as an author.
The Opéra dancers amused themselves
by encouraging his delusions, hailing
him as "*le grand Theleur*," and permitting
him to pick up the check at their
after-theatre suppers. They even
persuaded him to rent the Théâtre des
Folies-Dramatiques for a special
performance, where he made a grand
entrance in a chariot drawn by two
imitation tigers—his efforts to borrow live
ones from the Jardin des Plantes having
proved unsuccessful—and danced a *pas
seul* with roses in his hair. Apparently he
never suspected that his triumph was a
spurious one, and that the Opéra dancers
were choking with laughter as they
pelted him with flowers. But his *Letters
on Dancing* survives.

Exotic locales continued to stimulate the choreographic imagination. Giovanni Monticini used the discovery of Florida as the subject for a ballet given in Turin in 1803, while Jean Coralli, remembered now for *Giselle*, which he staged more than a quarter of a century later, produced a work called *The Incas* in Vienna in 1807. When William Barrymore, stage director of Drury Lane, the Royal Coburg, and other London theatres, was invited to produce a grand pantomime at the Teatro alla Canobbiana, Milan, in 1825, he chose for his theme the shipwreck of the French explorer LaPérouse, and presented what was probably a fairly close reproduction of the work which had been familiar on the London stage for twenty years. Alessandro Sanquirico, whose collaboration with Salvatore Viganò had been so fruitful, designed the superb settings for *Il Naufragio di La Perouse*. The one shown here is from a very fine aquatint by Carolina Lose.

Barrymore remained in Milan for a season, producing another pantomime, *Don Giovanni, ossia Il Dissoluto Punito*, early in 1826. Returning to London, he spent several years at Drury Lane before emigrating to America, where he remained for the rest of his life. His wife, the lovely Ann Adams Barrymore, was a popular performer in the graceful English style of dancing, which emphasized lyricism and femininity rather than technical prowess. She was especially admired for her performance as Fenella, the dumb girl of Portici, in Auber's opera-ballet *Masaniello*. She danced the role often in Boston, where the Barrymores settled not long after their arrival in the United States. After her retirement from the stage Mrs Barrymore opened a dancing school where she trained several accomplished American dancers, including Fanny Jones and Cecilia McBride.

The glamor, zest, and excitement of the Spanish dance have always made it a subject appealing to painters. This is one of the reasons why the Dance Collection, which makes a conscious effort to obtain full pictorial representation of ethnic as well as theatrical and social dances, is so rich in prints pertaining to the dances of the Iberian peninsula. A prime example is the aquatint of the bolero by T. Clark after William Bradford. Undated, it probably precedes the period when Fanny Elssler, with her dashing Cachucha, made Spanish dancing such a vivid and seductive element of the romantic ballet.

A charming print, which is also a document of enormous importance in the history of theatrical dancing, is the lithograph depicting Amalia Brugnoli and Jean Rozier in *Die Fee und Der Ritter*, choreographed by Armand Vestris and produced in Vienna in 1823. This picture is significant for two reasons: it is one of the first to show a ballerina supported by her partner in an adagio movement, and it portrays Brugnoli standing on the very tips, or pointes, of her toes. Pointe work was not the sudden invention of a single person. Since about 1800, perhaps even earlier, ballerinas had been rising higher and higher on the half pointe, until they discovered that it was possible to maintain the balance for brief poses on the tips of the toes. Dancers with strong feet and a fine sense of equilibrium began deliberately to cultivate the new achievement. It is known that Geneviève-Adelaide Gosselin, Teresa Ginetti, and Fanny Bias danced on pointe before 1820, but Amalia Brugnoli was one of the first ballerinas whose fame rested primarily on her amazing virtuosity in pointe work.

Marie Taglioni, often erroneously credited with the invention of this facet of technique, saw Brugnoli in Vienna when she herself was just a novice, and always remembered the dazzling footwork of the elder ballerina. Taglioni was to make dancing on pointe something more than an acrobatic accomplishment. She

nsmuted a simple feat into the symbol
poetry and romantic aspiration.

Born in Stockholm in 1804, Taglioni
de her debut in Vienna at eighteen.
ur years later, she appeared in
uttgart in her father's ballet *Jocko, or
e Brazilian Ape.* Taken from a
ntomime which had been popular in
ris in the preceding season, *Jocko* had
e exotic jungle locale still so much in
or. Audiences apparently found
thing incongruous about a South
merican Indian dancing on the pointes
her toes. *Jocko* featured the agile
tics of a man in a monkey suit, rather
an the delicate art of the young
llerina.

The Dance Collection's prints of *Jocko*
d *La Sonnambula* have a special value
cause they show the dancers in action
thin the stage scene, thus giving a far
earer understanding of the productions
the time than the more usual pictures
stage settings alone, or separate
rtraits of individual performers.

Modern ballet audiences know the
eme of the sleepwalker from George
lanchine's *La Sonnambula*, originally
lled *Night Shadow.* The subject was
ed more than a century earlier,
wever, by the choreographer Jean
amer, who presented his *La Somnambule*
the Paris Opéra in 1827. Enormously
ccessful, it soon appeared in the
pertoires of companies all over Europe,
d even in America.

The Dance Collection's engraving
ows the climax of the ballet as it was
esented in 1829 in Vienna, where the
ung Austrian ballerina Fanny Elssler
nced the title role. The major interest
the scene, although focused on the
gile figure of the sleepwalker
ecariously stepping along the edge of
e roof, is found in the dramatic reaction
the crowd assembled below. The scene
a vivid reminder of the balletic tradition
meaningful ensemble action, employed
th such a masterful hand by Michel
kine in *Petrouchka*, and preserved today

44, 45, 46, 47 The Dancing Lesson, *four caricatures by George Cruikshank*

L'Eté

The Dancing Lesson. Pt 3

G. Cruikshank fect.

Pubd by Thos McLean 26 Haymarket
Augt 1st 1835

The Sailors Hornpipe

The Dancing Lesson Pt 4

G. Cruikshank fect.

Pubd by Thos McLean 26 Haymarket
Augt 1st 1835

in the Royal Danish Ballet's productions of August Bournonville's *Napoli*, *Kermesse in Bruges*, and *A Folk Tale*.

Britain's distinguished satirist of the social scene, George Cruikshank, found dancing a congenial subject for his facile pencil. Born in 1792, he was familiar with the minuet and lived through the heyday of the quadrille, the waltz, and the polka. All of them fell victim to his devastating wit.

Although he was an extraordinarily prolific artist, Cruikshank in his youth seems to have spent almost as much time at the theatre and in the ballroom as he did over the drawing board. He loved to dance, and kept his health and suppleness so well that he was able to do a hornpipe at eighty-three, and prance through a sword dance, over poker and tongs, a year later.

The four plates of *The Dancing Lesson* reveal his affectionate understanding of the subject as well as his penetrating powers of observation. The extremely turned-out feet of both master and small pupil in *The First Position* show the influence of the classic ballet on social dancing as late as 1835. The youngsters of the aristocracy were still expected to acquire the artificial stance of the ballet dancer, even if it necessitated standing with one's feet in a box, like the plump little sufferer in the background of Plate 2, or forcing one's shoulders back by grasping a board, as in Plate 4. They learned the minuet, although it had long been a museum piece, and the enduring *pas d'été*. The boys, at least, could occasionally relax with a hornpipe.

By this time, however, it was the waltz which ruled the ballroom. Although he ignored it in *The Dancing Lesson*—perhaps because his small subjects were too young for its voluptuous measures—Cruikshank had a particular predilection for the waltz, and enjoyed sketching it in its more rowdy and athletic manifestations.

Anais Colin saw the waltz in quite a

45

different light, and in Sorrieu's lithogra[ph] from his drawing of the *valse à trois ten*[ps] the gentle and modest demeanor of th[e] dancing couple would certainly have earned the approval of Queen Victori[a] herself. As a matter of fact, the young Victoria was very fond of dancing, bot[h] in the ballroom and on the stage. She even collected ballet prints, several of which now belong to the Dance Collection.

Queen Victoria's favorite ballerina was Marie Taglioni, whose dancing wa[s] distinguished by its ethereal and spirit[ual] quality. Her art found its most perfec[t] expression in her father's ballet *La Sylphide*, created at the Paris Opéra i[n] 1832 and performed in London that same year. *La Sylphide* was the very essence of romanticism. This fresh an[d] vital spirit had made itself felt earlier [in] the century in music, painting, and poetry. *La Sylphide* marked the beginn[ing] of its ascendancy in the art of the dan[ce.] This was the first of the *ballets blancs*, those "white ballets" in which exquisit[e,] delicate creatures in diaphanous bell-shaped skirts float with imponder[able] lightness in moonlit landscapes. Examp[les] popular today are the second act of *Giselle, Les Sylphides* (Michel Fokine's tribute to the romantic period), and, [of] course, *La Sylphide* itself. Preserved f[or] more than a century in the repertoire [of] the Royal Danish Ballet (in a version [by] August Bournonville), it has been produced in the 1960s by Ballet Rambe[rt,] the American Ballet Theatre, and the National Ballet of Canada. Unlike its fragile heroine, it seems destined for immortality.

The story of *La Sylphide* concerns a[n] young Scotsman, James, who falls in l[ove] with a spirit of the air. Taglioni's miraculous dancing of the title role, in which her delicate pointe work gave t[he] actual illusion of flight, was the inspiration of countless painters and sculptors. The ballet's opening tablea[u,] with the Sylphide kneeling beside the

sleeping James, was painted by Georges Lepaulle, and promptly reproduced by the American lithographers Edmund B. and Elijah C. Kellogg of Hartford, Connecticut, in a print which is now one of the rarest in the Dance Collection.

The scene a moment later, when the Sylphide hovers behind James's chair, is the first in a series of six lithographs based on paintings by the English artist Alfred E. Chalon. Assembled in a handsome portfolio, they were issued together in 1845 to commemorate Taglioni's first farewell performances in London. (She did not actually retire until 1847.) The second of the Chalon lithographs shows the Sylphide in the window, mourning James's bethrothal to his childhood sweetheart, Effie. In another, she is poised so lightly on the tips of her toes that she really seems to be supported by her gossamer wings. In a fourth, having persuaded James to desert Effie and follow her into her forest domain, she pauses on a slender branch to show him the nest of a bird, a sister creature of the air.

James is a mortal, and although the Sylphide loves him she constantly flies from his human grasp. An evil witch gives James a magic scarf with which to ensnare her. When he twines it around her shoulders, her wings drop off and she dies. The two final pictures show the falling of the wings, and Taglioni's gracious acknowledgement of the ovation which invariably followed her performance in *La Sylphide*.

As the most celebrated dancer of her century, Taglioni inspired dozens of painters and lithographers, but none succeeded in suggesting the imponderable lightness of her dancing more effectively than Chalon in this farewell tribute. Although separate prints from it turn up occasionally, the complete portfolio is rare indeed, and the Dance Collection is extremely fortunate in possessing an example of it.

51, 52, 53, 54, 55 *Marie Taglioni in La Sylphide as drawn by Alfred E. Chalon in 1845*

Entered according to Act of Congress in the Year 1836 by H.R. Robinson, in the Clerks Office of the District Court of the United States of the Southern District of New York.

THE CELESTE-AL CABINET.

DICKENSON.	BUTLER.	CASS.	JIMMY O'NEAL. Door Keeper.	CELESTE.	GENERAL JACKSON.	KENDAL.	WOODBURY.	VANBUREN.

Published April 1836 by H.R. Robinson 48 Courtlandt St. N.Y.

ot even the incomparable Taglioni was
afe from caricature. If this goddess of
he dance suffered from the lampoons of
atirists who made fun of her slenderness,
er modesty, and her demure expression,
esser luminaries were far more
ulnerable. In the United States, in
articular, they sometimes suffered from
he harsh ridicule they received in prints
hich seem merely amusing and
nteresting to us now, but were misleading
nd even cruel at the time of their
ppearance.

Ballet had been introduced in the
nited States shortly after the American
evolution. It had enjoyed a mild and
ntermittent popularity until the 1830s,
hen the advent of European ballerinas
f stature, and the development of
merican dancers in the schools of
hilip Hazard, a former member of the
aris Opéra ensemble, and Ann Adams
arrymore, a graduate of the London
tage, gave the art a strong impetus.
nhanced by the newly developed
echnique of dancing on the pointes and
he attractiveness of romantic themes,
allet gradually assumed a position of
mportance in the American theatre.

One of the most glamorous of the
mported dancers was Mlle Celeste (born
eleste Keppler), who arrived in New
ork in 1827. Barely sixteen, she was a
omparative novice, but her Paris Opéra
raining plus a brilliant talent for mime
nd a tremendous flair for the theatre
oon made her a star of the first
agnitude. One of the first to dance on
ointe in the United States, she excelled
n *pirouettes* and other *tours de force*, but
as especially distinguished by the
ramatic talent which enabled her in
ter years to become a first-rate actress.
It was Celeste who first brought an
xcerpt from *La Sylphide* to America, in
835, but the ethereal role did not suit
er robust personality, and she never
anced the complete ballet here. More to
er taste were such *travesti* mime roles
that of the Wild Arab Boy, where she

revelled in the opportunity to play havoc
with the emotions of the spectators while
generously exhibiting her well-rounded
legs.

During her second tour of the United
States Celeste is said to have attracted
the favorable attention of President
Andrew Jackson, whose weakness for
pretty ladies had already embroiled him
in difficulties more than once. At any
rate, during the presidential campaign
of 1836, when Jackson's follower Martin
Van Buren was running against both
William Henry Harrison and Daniel
Webster, the well-known political
caricaturist Henry R. Robinson used an
imaginary scene in the White House,
with the charming French ballerina
performing for the President and his
"Celeste-Al Cabinet," as a form of
anti-Jacksonian propaganda.

Except with the rabid minority, it
probably did Celeste no harm to find her
name linked with that of the President
of the United States. Eugenie LeComte,
on the other hand, nearly suffered
professional ostracism because of the
bare-bosomed "portrait" of her circulated
by Robinson. Mme LeComte had enjoyed
a fairly impressive career in France,
England, Italy, and even in Russia before
she came to America in 1837. She made
her debut at the Park Theatre, New York,
as the Abbess Helena in Meyerbeer's
opera-ballet *Robert the Devil*, in which
she led an infernal ballet of renegade
nuns. It is quite certain, however, that
she did not do so in the totally topless
costume depicted in the Robinson print.
Perhaps the whole affair of "the
prosecuted picture" was instigated by
a professional rival.

Mme LeComte survived the scandal to
tour the country several times. It was
she who brought Marius Petipa to
America for a brief and unlucky season
in 1839. It was a financial disaster, and
the future choreographer of *Swan Lake*
made only a few appearances in New
York before scurrying back to Europe.

57   *Celeste as the Arab Boy*

58   *Eugenie LeComte*

The ballerina of the century, for the American public, was the glorious Fanny Elssler. She not only made a profound artistic impression—Ralph Waldo Emerson and Margaret Fuller were among her admirers—but she created a furore which found expression in all sorts of tangible souvenirs of her triumphant progress around the country. Dozens of music sheets appeared, each containing the accompaniment to one of her favorite dances and bearing her lithographed portrait on the cover. Her likeness was embossed in glass on whiskey bottles, and pressed in crude but curiously attractive little metal gilt figurines which still turn up, occasionally in lamps or girandoles. James Varick Stout carved a life-size statue of her, and amassed a small fortune by exhibiting it for an admission fee of twenty-five cents.

Nathaniel Currier, who later formed half of the famous printmaking firm of Currier and Ives, was a balletomane and a particular admirer of Elssler's. He published more than a dozen prints and music covers depicting the fascinating artist in the Cracovienne, the Cachucha, the Zapateado and the other colorful and exhilarating dances she made so distinctly her own. One of his most successful publications (based on a European original by Lejeune) was *The Three Graces*, a blatant piece of Elssler propaganda. It places her prominently front and center, at the resplendent zenith of her career, while the aging Taglioni fades into the background and the young Fanny Cerrito turns her head covetously towards the spotlight.

Elssler was indeed at the very peak of her powers during her two-year American tour, 1840–1842. Born in Vienna in 1810, she had already conquered the discriminating audiences of Paris, Berlin and London before she came to the United States. At thirty, she was noted for the precision and virtuosity of her dancing, which encompassed pointe work more intricate than anything

eviously attempted. However, it was
r extraordinary beauty, the eloquence
her acting, and the intoxicating warmth
her stage presence which set her apart
om other dancers. She was the very
tithesis of Taglioni, who danced like
disembodied spirit; Elssler was a
agnificent specimen of womanhood.
During her sojourn in this country,
ssler did much to encourage American
ncers. Julia Turnbull, Fanny Jones,
eorge Washington Smith, Henry and
arriet Wells, and the four Vallee sisters
danced in her company from time to
ne. Unfortunately the lovely Cecilia
cBride, a pupil of Ann Adams
rrymore, contracted tuberculosis and
the time of Elssler's visit was no
nger able to dance. She struggled on
r several years as an actress, and died
Boston, the city of her birth, in 1846.
ndleton's charming lithograph is the
ly surviving souvenir of her brief
reer.
Fanny Elssler, on the other hand,
valled Taglioni in the number and
uality of the art works she inspired.
er Cachucha was captured in an
xcellent bronze by Barre, now in the
ance Collection, which also has a fine
sque statuette of her in the same dance.
nortly after her New York debut,
hich took place at the Park Theatre on
ay 14, 1840, the noted American artist
enry Inman persuaded Elssler to sit
r him. She posed at the theatre, seated
fore her dressing table, and wearing
e white costume of the bridal scene in
a Tarentule, the ballet she had danced
n her opening night. Elssler was so
eased with the portrait that she took it
ick to Vienna with her, but before her
eparture she permitted a still more
lebrated painter, Thomas Sully, to
opy it. Perhaps best known for his
andsome portrait of the young Queen
ictoria, which hangs in the Pennsylvania
useum of Fine Arts, Philadelphia,
ully was a pupil of Benjamin West. The
n of Matthew Sully, a popular actor-

60 *Cecilia McBride*

dancer and mime, the future painter was a dancer at the Charleston Theatre in his youth, and had his first drawing lessons from his brother-in-law, Jean Belzons, who designed the scenery there.

The Inman painting of Fanny Elssler is now in the Haydn Museum at Eisenstadt, Austria, with other mementos of the ballerina's career. (Her father was Haydn's music copyist.) Thomas Sully's version, so glowingly alive that it must be considered a superb example of that master's art, is one of the most highly prized possessions of the Dance Collection, and serves as the frontispiece to this book. With the generous cooperation of its previous owner, George Chaffee, it was acquired and presented to the Library by the Friends of the Dance Collection.

The lithograph of Paul and Amelie Taglioni, drawn by Napoleon Sarony and published by Robinson, celebrates their American debut. This performance, at the Park Theatre, New York, on May 22, 1839, was also the occasion of the first complete production of *La Sylphide* in this country. Paul Taglioni, brother of the more famous Marie, had been her partner when she danced her favorite role in Berlin and London in 1832, the year of its creation. On those occasions his German wife, born Amelie Galster, had played Effie, the young fiancée of the hero, James. More recently, however, Amelie Taglioni had assumed the title role at the Berlin Royal Opera, where her husband was ballet master and *premier danseur*.

Fragments of *La Sylphide* had been presented on the American stage intermittently ever since Mlle Celeste had introduced a solo excerpt from it in 1835. An opera called *The Mountain Sylph*, composed by John Barnett and based on the same libretto as the ballet, had enjoyed a mild success in the United States. Augusta Maywood, then only thirteen years old and known as *la petite Augusta*, had appeared in an arrangement

in which the Sylphide's role was danced and the other principal parts were sung. Several other ballerinas, including young Harriet Wells, Mme LeComte, and Augusta St James (known on the stage simply as Mme Augusta) had starred in this hybrid version. Not until the arrival of the Taglionis, however, was the original staging seen or the Schneitzhoeffer score heard in America.

In the authentic choreography of Filippo Taglioni, with which his son Paul was of course thoroughly familiar, *La Sylphide* had a triumphant success. Amelie Taglioni (who seems to have been a lyric, poetic dancer, of the same type as her sister-in-law) was praised for effortless lightness and dexterity. Paul was compared to a race horse in his clean, sinewy muscularity. Although Charles Vestris, nephew of the great Auguste, had appeared in the United States in 1829, since then there had been no male dancer to approach Paul Taglioni. His dancing was a revelation.

Once firmly established in the American theatre, *La Sylphide* retained its popularity until the Civil War interrupted the normal course of theatrical activity. Among the ballerinas who performed it were Mary Ann Lee (remembered as the first American *Giselle*), the Philadelphia dancer Henrietta Vallee, Hermine Blangy of the Paris Opéra, the Italian Teresa Rolla, and Yrca Matthias, a French dancer who earned fame in Russia.

The most illustrious Sylphide ever to dance the role in America, however, was Fanny Elssler, who arrived the year after the Taglionis completed their single summer season here. In Paris, where she had been obliged to face direct comparison with Marie Taglioni, Elssler's Sylphide had been a comparative failure. Critical observers felt, perhaps with some justification, that she was far better suited to those exhilarating character dances she performed with such vivacity. In the United States, however, her

interpretation was appreciated for its
own distinctive merits. In the final scen
where the Sylphide loses her wings an
her immortality, Elssler's mime was so
touching that the most hardened Yank
sceptics melted in tears.

The brilliance of Elssler's dancing is
vividly suggested in a lithograph by
Gauci after J. Deffett Francis, which
shows her in the forgotten ballet *La
Volière*. The artist has caught her in
motion. She seems to be turning in the
air, her filmy skirts flying, a gossamer v
swirling above her shoulders, her arche
feet stretching downward in a flawless
position which still conveys the illusio
of spontaneity.

While Elssler was invading Taglioni
territory by dancing *La Sylphide*, her
rival was reciprocating by appearing a
gypsy girl in the ballet *La Gitana*, whi
her father had created for her in Russi
in 1839. She danced the role two years
later in Milan, where Roberto Focosi
recorded her performance in an unusua
beautiful lithograph. She seems the
personification of lightness and grace.
But if one took away the tambourine a
added a pair of wings, she might easily
appear to be dancing *La Sylphide*. The
flashing eyes and voluptuous abandon
the gypsy seem to have eluded the
decorous Taglioni.

In the meantime, a younger and less
spiritual Sylphide had been attracting
considerable attention. Her 1841
appearances in Milan had preceded
Taglioni's by just a few weeks. Born in
Naples in 1817, Fanny Cerrito was a
sunny child of the south. She had
abundant energy and a radiant smile;
where Taglioni floated, she bounced.
Her infectious charm made the sternes
critics forget the deficiencies of her
technique. Why should anyone quibbl
about precision and neatness when
Cerrito could spin so swiftly and dart
about the stage with such reckless
assurance?

In London in 1842 Cerrito found a ro

Fanny Cerrito in La Sylphide   *64   Marie Taglioni in* La Gitana, *1841*   57

which suited her to perfection. In *Alma, the Daughter of Fire*, she played the part of a statue given life on condition that she never fall in love. Guided by the demon Periphete (Jules Perrot), Alma undergoes all sorts of tests before she succumbs to the ardor of the Moorish prince Emazir and is turned back to stone. The Dance Collection's water color shows the *Pas de Fascination* in which, urged on by Periphete, the irresistible Alma enchants the entire population of a German village. Unsigned, the drawing is probably R. J. Hamerton's original for the lithograph issued by William Spooner in 1842. *Dancing in Prints*, the portfolio of reproductions published by the Library in 1964 to celebrate the twentieth anniversary of the Dance Collection, includes another fine lithograph, by Bouvier, depicting Cerrito in the same dance.

An unsolved mystery concerns the album of costume sketches which include the design for Marie Taglioni's costume in *Herta*, a ballet her father produced for her in Russia in 1842. This particular water color bears Marie Taglioni's own autograph signature, as does one other drawing in the little book. Did it ever belong to her? A fascinating project is waiting for the right scholar, in the study of this collection of designs.

Esmeralda, based on Victor Hugo's *Notre Dame de Paris*, was a superb example of Jules Perrot's choreography in which brilliant dancing and expressive mime were inextricably blended. Bouvier's lithograph shows Perrot dancing the *Truandaise* with Carlotta Grisi, the young Italian dancer who had recently created the title role of *Giselle*. In Grisi were united all the best attributes of the other outstanding ballerinas of the romantic period: the buoyant elevation of Taglioni, the technical virtuosity and mimic powers of Elssler, and the joyous exuberant facility of Cerrito. If she could not claim to surpass her peers in any one aspect of her art, Grisi

65   *Costume for Marie Taglioni in* Herta   66   *Fanny Cerrito in* Alma

outstripped them all in versatility. *Gise[lle]*
gave full scope to every facet of her tale[nts.]
The first act, with its mad scene, deman[ds]
an actress of consummate ability; the
second (where the betrayed heroine h[as]
been transformed into a Wili), a danc[er]
capable of suggesting the imponderab[le]
lightness of a disembodied spirit. Becau[se]
it requires such a consummate master[y]
of the whole range of classical dancing,
Giselle is still considered the touchsto[ne]
of the ballerina's art. Danced in recen[t]
years by such memorable interpreters [as]
Alicia Alonso, Margot Fonteyn, Alicia
Markova, and Galina Ulanova, the rol[e]
still indelibly linked with the name of
Carlotta Grisi, for whom it was create[d.]

Giselle was first performed at the Pa[ris]
Opéra on June 28, 1841. The libretto,
based on a German legend related by
Heinrich Heine, was written by Grisi'[s]
ardent admirer, Théophile Gautier; th[e]
score was composed by Adolphe Ada[m.]
Jean Coralli was credited with the
choreography, but he undoubtedly
received considerable assistance from
Perrot, who was Grisi's discoverer,
teacher, and husband. Lucien Petipa
created the role of Albrecht, which ha[s]
been danced so nobly in our time by E[rik]
Bruhn, Henning Kronstam, and Igor
Youskevitch. The first Myrtha, Quee[n of]
the Wilis, was Adele Dumilâtre, who
appeared in the same part in London t[wo]
years later when Fanny Elssler, on he[r]
return from America, danced Giselle.

The clean lines of Dumilâtre's
arabesque in Bouvier's lithograph
graphically convey the cold, clear-cut
character of the role of the Wili Quee[n.]
Dumilâtre was a dark-haired beauty w[ho]
briefly challenged the recognized star[s of]
the romantic ballet in Paris and Lond[on]
without ever attaining their celestial
heights. She did, however, inspire sev[eral]
unusually attractive prints, and Bouvi[er]
in particular seems to have found her [an]
appealing subject.

From the ballet academy at La Scal[a,]
Milan, where Carlo Blasis and his wif[e]

been teaching for some years, there
an to emerge at about this time the
guard of the long procession of Italian
erinas who were to rule the stage for
rly half a century. They were
lliant technicians, who could perform
sorts of dazzling and previously
attempted feats on their toes. Blasis'
pils were particularly adept at
ouettes and turns of all kinds, for he
d apparently discovered the trick of
pping the head at a faster rhythm
n that of the body, which keeps the
ncer from getting dizzy.

Blasis was especially proud "of seven
ncers whom he called his Pleiades."
ese were Marietta Baderna, Augusta
minechettis, Amalia Ferraris, Sofia
oco, Flora Fabbri, Carolina Granzini,
d one man, Pasquale Borri. In his
tes Upon Dancing, published in
ndon in 1847, Blasis described the
dividual characteristics and listed the
ofessional triumphs of these favorites.

Among the first to acquire international
ebrity was Flora Fabbri, who made her
ndon debut at Drury Lane Theatre in
e autumn of 1845, dancing the role of
azourka, a basket maker's wife, in
seph Mazilier's ballet *The Devil to Pay*.
e part had been created by Carlotta
isi earlier that same year, at the Paris
éra. It required a fine sense of comedy
well as no little virtuosity, but Fabbri,
the English production, succeeded in
king it very much her own. She
peared at the Paris Opéra intermittently
m 1845 to 1851, and toured widely in
ly and Germany. According to Blasis,
diences were invariably entranced by
e joyous and ardent spirit of her
ncing.

Marietta Baderna, born in 1830, was
ly sixteen years old when Giuliani's
usual lithograph of her was published
Milan. It shows her surrounded by
teen miniature figures representing
r various roles. Poses from *Giselle* and
Sylphide are recognizable, and
parently Baderna was adept at the

70 *Marietta Baderna, 1846*

rious Polish, Spanish, and Russian
nces which Fanny Elssler had made so
pular. For such a youthful artist, her
pertoire was amazingly extensive. When
rlo Blasis accepted an engagement as
est choreographer at Drury Lane,
rly in 1847, he took Baderna along to
erpret the leading roles in the ballets
produced there. Critics praised her
ely arms and strong pointe work. They
nd, however, that Blasis seemed
able to develop a dramatic theme,
hough he staged effective dances and
vertissements.

Baderna was one of the first classic
ncers to visit South America. In 1850
e appeared in Rio de Janeiro, where
e was lucky enough to escape the
vages of a yellow fever epidemic which
led 16,000 people, including her own
her.

The most distinguished of all Blasis'
pils was Amalia Ferraris. Her technique
s prodigious. She could leap like a
vn, and descend as gently as a falling
af. The strength of her pointe work
s astonishing, and she is said to have
en able to balance on the tip of one
e on the narrow side of a tambourine.
Born at Voghera, Italy, in 1830, she
s a star at Her Majesty's Theatre,
ndon, by the time she was twenty.
ere she competed successfully with
ch established artists as Fanny Cerrito
d Carlotta Grisi. Later she ruled for
ven years as prima ballerina at the
ris Opéra, and in 1858 made her
but in St Petersburg, where Jules
rrot produced his *Eoline* for her. The
arming lithograph by Marcovich
cords a delightful pose (typical of the
riod) which occurs also in the *pas de
ux* from August Bournonville's *Flower
stival in Genzano*, still danced today.

Giovannina King was not one of
asis's "Pleiades," but she was his
pil. Her earliest training, however,
s received under Pietro Hus in Naples,
r birthplace, and she also studied
der Bournonville's pupil Gustave

73 *A Neapolitan tarantella*

ey. (Her pose, like that of Ferraris, is
iniscent of the Danish master.) Most
er career was spent in Italy, and she
ced with enormous success from one
of the peninsula to the other. The
rce of her English name remains a
stery.

ofia Fuoco, like Ferraris, was a
erina di forza. Her pointe work was
vellous. She was probably one of the
dancers to turn pirouettes on pointe.
he very soft, unboxed satin slippers
n during the romantic period such a
would have required amazing
ngth and control, but Fuoco seems
ave accomplished it.

orn in Milan in 1830, Fuoco entered
ballet academy at La Scala when she
seven. She made her debut at the
is Opéra at sixteen, and her triumphs
re were followed by splendid seasons
ondon and Madrid. In Italy her
cing aroused such fanatical
nusiasm that not even a cholera
lemic, which was raging in Perugia
ing her engagement there in 1856,
ld keep people away from the theatre.
uoco made the national dance of her
ntry, the spirited tarantella, an
xicating theatrical experience, and
finest portrait is probably the
ograph by Sanesi which shows her
cing it. A shining example of this
ning Italian dance is the climax of the
al Danish Ballet's wonderful *Napoli*,
ch August Bournonville produced
r a visit to Naples in 1841. Perhaps
rought back to Copenhagen a copy
he enchanting little book of
ographs by Gaetano Dura illustrating
steps and positions of the tarantella,
directions for dancing it by Pasquale
odi. Its frontispiece shows a
ement which Bournonville
roduced in the last act of his great
et. The tarantella is still an inspiration
horeographers; George Balanchine
ted a sparkling one for Patricia
Bride and Edward Villella in 1963.
t of the Dance Collection's superb

74 *Sofia Fuoco in a tarantella*

75 Pas de Quatre (*Taglioni, Grisi, Cerrito, Grahn*), 1845

gallery of Italian ballet prints belong to the Cia Fornaroli Collection, and were lovingly assembled by the ballerina and her husband. They were the donors, as well, of Brandard's striking picture of the memorable *Pas de Quatre* of 1845.

This unique divertissement has often been called the apogee of the romantic ballet. In it appeared four of the greatest dancers of that or any other period.

During the summer of 1845 Marie Taglioni, Fanny Cerrito, Carlotta Grisi, and the young Danish dancer Lucile Grahn were all simultaneously engaged at Her Majesty's Theatre, London. The enterprising impresario, Benjamin Lumley, conceived the daring idea of having them perform together in a single brief ballet, a *Pas de Quatre* of such brilliance that nothing remotely approaching it had ever been attempted before. Since the four stars were, of course, bitter rivals, it required diplomacy of the highest order to persuade them to agree to such an unprecedented proposition.

Agree they did, and Jules Perrot set to work to create a series of dances which would display the most scintillating talents of each ballerina, without giving predominance to any one of the four. All went smoothly until the final rehearsal, when the entire project nearly collapsed over the question of the order of the solo variations. The coveted privilege of dancing last had been given to Taglioni, by unanimous consent, and the comparatively unknown Grahn had agreed to be first. But Cerrito absolutely would not dance before Grisi, and Grisi just as adamantly refused to precede Cerrito. Lumley's arbitration of the affair produced a judgement worthy of Solomon: the eldest, he proclaimed, should of course have the preferred position. Cerrito, two years older than her compatriot, was more than a little reluctant to claim her victory!

Perrot's choreography must have been masterly, for it achieved an harmonious unity while permitting each ballerina to enjoy a personal triumph in steps exactly suited to her own individual style. At the first performance on July 12, 1845, the entrance of each dancer brought down a veritable hailstorm of bouquets, and at the final curtain the stage was all but buried under an avalanche of flowers.

The *Pas de Quatre* was danced only three more times that summer. Queen Victoria attended the third performance, and her proof copy of Maguire's well known lithograph of the ballet (after Alfred E. Chalon) has been reproduced in the Library's publication, *Dancing in Prints*. John Brandard's attractive study, shown here, is less familiar. It once decorated the cover of an excerpt from Cesare Pugni's delightful score, known today through recordings and through the reconstructions of the ballet choreographed in recent times by Keith Lester and Anton Dolin.

Lucile Grahn, youngest of the ballerinas of the *Pas de Quatre*, was born in Copenhagen in 1819. The favorite pupil and protegée of August Bournonville, she had an aerial lightness reminiscent of Taglioni. It was Grahn who created the title role in Bournonville's version of *La Sylphide*, first produced at the Royal Danish Theatre in 1836.

Bournonville ruled his company with an iron hand. Grahn, a strong-minded young woman with a will of her own, frequently clashed with him, especially after a successful debut at the Paris Opéra in 1838 had given her a taste of independence. When she wished to introduce Fanny Elssler's Cachucha at the Royal Theatre, the dictatorial ballet master was furious; when, to show off her sparkling footwork, she changed some of the steps in his ballet *Valdemar*, he made a formal protest to the directors of the theatre.

Early in 1839, Grahn obtained permission to accept a brief guest engagement in Hamburg. There her triumph was sensational. Intoxicated by

the adulation she received from the
cordial German public, she applied fo
prolongation of her leave of absence.
When her request was peremptorily
denied, she simply stayed in Hambur
anyway. A few weeks later she was
dismissed from the Royal Danish Bal
She never danced in Copenhagen aga
Throughout the rest of Europe, howe
her career was prosperous and prolon;
She spent her final years in Munich,
ballet mistress of the Hofoper, and w
she died in 1907 she left her consider
fortune to that municipality. In gratitu
the city named a street for her. Thro
all the vicissitudes of changing regim
it has remained the Lucile Grahn Stra

Not one of the ballerinas of the *Pas
Quatre* ever danced in America, altho
from time to time there were active
rumors of projected tours by almost :
of them, and Fanny Cerrito came ver
close to accepting an offer to appear
Niblo's Garden, New York, in 1855.
After Fanny Elssler's fabulous conqu
ballet remained for more than a doze
years one of the most powerful attract
in the American theatre. If the great
stars failed to profit from this situatic
a number of lesser luminaries surely

Hermine Blangy was a graduate of
Paris Opéra. Trained in its school, sl
had risen through the ranks until in
1840 she was dancing the title role o
La Sylphide there. She also appeared
the Queen of the Wilis in *Giselle*. Fo
three years she was prima ballerina a
the Hofoper in Vienna, and in 1846
came to the United States. The balle
she danced in New York, and on the
tours which took her as far as Havan
and New Orleans, included *La Sylph
Le Diable Boiteux* (the work in which
Elssler had first performed her alluri
Cachucha), Perrot's *L'Illusion d'un
Peintre*, and *La Fille de Marbre* (a
version of *Alma*). In *Giselle* she was
successful that in 1847 she could dai
it ten times in a fortnight in Mobile,
Alabama, which certainly had not th

tained the population of 200,000 it
n claim today. During an engagement
 New Orleans in 1846, she challenged
mparison with the American ballerina
ary Ann Lee, who had introduced
iselle to the United States earlier that
me year, by dancing the role in one
eatre at the same time that Lee was
pearing in it at another. Some
nnoisseurs preferred the interpretation
 the Philadelphia girl, while others
varded the palm to the foreign
llerina.

The handsome portrait of Blangy is
 untitled example of a lithograph by
harles Currier (brother of Nathaniel, of
rrier and Ives fame) after Francis
avignon and Joseph Vollmering. It
ows her in the second act of *Giselle.*
he original drawing has been attributed
 Davignon, who was responsible for a
ndful of the very finest American
llet prints, including the Dance
ollection's stunning lithograph of
iovanna Ciocca.

Nathalie Fitzjames danced at the Paris
péra with Hermine Blangy, and left it
 about the same time, to tour in Italy.
e was especially admired in Naples. In
e autumn of 1850 she came to the
nited States as ballerina of an opera
mpany directed by the noted
presario Max Maretzek, and made her
but at the Astor Place Opera House in
quita, staged for her by Lucien
tipa. Although American audiences
preciated her proficiency, she was
uch too thin for their taste (even in
ris she had been compared to an
paragus) and they also thought her
st her prime. The spring of 1851
und her in strange company, appearing
 Brooklyn with a "Bloomer Troupe"
nich was exploiting the recently
vented and decidedly audacious
stume for women. The Dance
ollection's lovely lithograph, with the
e of the dancer's flying arabesque
peated in her diaphanous scarf, recalls
r earlier career.

77 *Hermine Blangy in* Giselle

During her Italian engagements Fitzjames, like so many other dancers of renown, burnished her technique in the Milan studio of Carlo Blasis. If he attracted dancers from all over the world he also disseminated them to its farthest corners. Giovanna Ciocca arrived in the United States in 1847, and promptly stirred up a hornet's nest by dancing the polka with such fascinating skill that her American partner, George Washington Smith, was no longer interested in executing the popular dance with his usual stage companion, Julia Turnbull. His refusal to do so caused a near-riot at the Bowery Theatre, where the ebullient "Bowery boys" nearly tore up the benches in protest. He was finally obliged to dance the polka four times (twice with each ballerina)!

The Bohemian polka had swept across Europe like wildfire in 1844, reaching American shores in the same year. It monopolized the ballroom, and after an enchanting version had been performed by Carlotta Grisi and Jules Perrot in London, it bade fair to take possession of the stage as well. Its hold on public favor was tenacious; in 1855 Pasquale Borri (the only man in Carlo Blasis's "Pleiades") staged a lively Redowa Polka for Pia Ricci, Henri Frappart, and Lorenzo Vienna, leading dancers of the Vienna Opera, where he was ballet master.

From Vienna, in 1845, came the *Petit Danseuses Viennoises*, a company of children drilled with such meticulous exactitude that they might be called the first "precision dancers," the predecessors of yesterday's Tiller Girls and today's Rockettes. They played guest engagements at the Paris Opéra, where the correctness of their geometrical evolutions put the resident ensemble to shame, and in London, where their winning and innocent demeanor charmed everyone, including the Queen. Their long tour of the United States, 1847 to

Harvest Dance of the Viennese children   *80   Redowa Polka*

81 *Polish Dance*

49, brought golden rewards to their
[bal]let-mistress-cum-manager, Mme
[Jo]sephine Weiss, and to theatre owners
[all] over the country.

One of their most effective numbers
[wa]s the Harvest Dance, in which they
[wield]ed small scythes and manoeuvred
[l]ong sheaves of wheat. Their
[ap]pearances no doubt awakened
[co]nsiderable nostalgia among the central
[Eu]ropeans who were beginning to pour
[int]o the United States in a rising flood
[of] immigration. Print sellers were ready
[to] capitalize on the longing for homelands
[by] providing attractive scenes from the
[old] countries; the vigorous *Polish Dance*,
[alt]hough published in Berlin, was
[wi]dely distributed by the New York
[firm] of Jacoby and Zeller.

Just such a Polish dance was to be
[ad]apted to the stage and featured, a few
[ye]ars later, in Leo Delibes' ballet
[Co]ppélia. In fact, the moment caught in
[th]e lithograph might almost be the
[op]ening of the first-act Mazurka. The en-
[rich]ment of theatrical dance from folk
[sou]rces still continues today.

The Italian tarantella, so often an
[ins]piration to ballet masters, was a
[hig]hlight of *L'Etoile de Messine*, the ballet
[wit]h which Pasquale Borri made his
[ch]oreographic debut at the Paris Opéra
[in] 1861. Its leading dancer was his
[col]league and compatriot Amalia Ferraris,
[wh]o found in the tragic role of the
[tru]sting and deceived heroine, Gazella,
[th]e opportunity for dramatic expression
[to] match her phenomenal technique. The
[rea]l star of *L'Etoile de Messine* was the
[en]semble, however, and the exceptional
[int]erest of the lithograph lies in the
[viv]id clarity with which it suggests the
[ent]ire stage picture and action.

[M]eanwhile another Italian, the
[cel]ebrated mime and choreographer
[Do]menico Ronzani, had brought to the
[Un]ited States the largest and perhaps
[th]e finest ballet company yet to arrive on
[the]se shores. Organized in Europe for
[the] express purpose of the American

tour, the Ronzani Ballet had been engaged to inaugurate the new Philadelphia Academy of Music, which is still, more than a century after it opened its doors, one of the most imposing theatres in the country. The leading dancers were Louise Lamoureux and Filippo Baratti, the principal mimes Cesare and Serafina Cecchetti. Their seven-year-old son Enrico, future great pedagogue, teacher of Pavlova and Nijinsky, was on hand to play the urchin in *Il Biricchino di Parigi*.

It was Ronzani's production of Jules Perrot's *Faust* which was presented on the opening night, September 15, 1857. The Dance Collection's impressive lithograph may show a scene from this ballet. Probably used as a poster (it is very large, more than two feet in width), it conveys a graphic impression of the formal, decorative use of the ensemble and the airy brilliance of the stars.

The American tour of the Ronzani company marked one of the last noteworthy manifestations of the romantic ballet in this country. After the Civil War such spectacular shows as *The Black Crook* attracted a flurry of interest, but the emphasis had passed from poetic quality to mechanical display.

At the same time, photography was beginning to replace engraving as a means of recording the fleeting images of the dance. The daguerreotype had been invented before Fanny Elssler visited America. Increasing use of the new medium, combined with a gradual decline of interest in the dance towards the end of the century, led to a profound change in the visual records of all kinds of dancing. With the twentieth-century renaissance, as new forms evolved, new ways to capture them on paper and canvas developed. But the historical treasures preserved by the Dance Collection are more than merely beautiful and priceless souvenirs of vanished arts and social customs; they are the raw material which can stimulate and nourish fresh creation.

83   The Ronzani Ballet

The Illustrations

The actual image area of each illustration has been measured. The dimensions of the prints are given in inches and sixteenths of inches, height preceding width. The height of each book is given in centimeters.

Frontispiece Fanny Elssler

Fanny Elssler in her dressing room at the Park Theatre, New York. Oil painting by Thomas Sully after Henry Inman, 28×23.12. Friends of the Dance Collection. From the George Chaffee Collection

1 *A seventeenth-century dancing school*

Engraved illustration on title page of: The Dancing-Master:/ Or, Directions for Dancing Country Dances, with the Tunes to each Dance for the Treble-Violin./ The Twelfth Edition, containing above 350 of the choicest Old and New Tunes now used at Court, and other Publick Places./ The whole Work Revised and much more Correct than any former Editions./ The Dancing Schoole./ Printed by J. Heppinstall for H. Playford at his Shop in the Temple-Change, or at his House in Arundel-street in the Strand, 1703/ Price Bound 3s.6d./ [by John Playford] 10.5 cm. Purchase Fund

2 Ballet Comique de la Reine

3 *The Four Cardinal Virtues*

Engraved illustrations to: Balet Comique/ de la Royne, faict/ avx nopces de Mon-/ sieur le Duc de Ioyeuse & madamoyselle de Vau-/ demont sa soeur./ [written in ink: Presenté par gentilshomes/ et Dames: et com-/ pose/ P] Baltasar de Beavioyevlx,/ valet de chambre dv/ Roy, & de la Royne sa mere./ A Paris,/ Par Adrian le Roy, Robert Ballard & Mamert/ Patisson, Imprimeurs du Roy./ M.D.LXXXII./ Avec Privilege./ [written in ink at top right: Tanquam/ In the middle of the page: Sum Ben: Jonsonij/ At lower left, the bookplate of Horace Walpole. At lower right, the bookplate of Sir Henry Brooke] 24 cm. Drexel Collection, from the library of Horace Walpole and presumed to have been the property of Ben Jonson

4 *Two dancers from Caroso's* Il Ballarino

Engraved illustration to: Il Ballarino/ di M. Fabritio Caroso/ da Sermoneta,/ Diviso in due Trattati;/ Ornato di molte Figure,/ Et con l'Intauolatura di Liuto, & il Soprano della Musica/ nella sonata di ciascun Ballo./ . . . In Venetia, Appresso Francesco Zanetti. MDLXXXI/ 24 cm. The Astor Library

5 *Cesare Negri's dance* L › Spagnoletto

Engraved illustration to: Le Gratie/ d'Amore,/ di Cesare Negri Milanese,/ detto Il Trombone Professore di ballare,/ opera nova, et vaghissima,/ divisa in tre trattati./ . . . in Milano,/ Per l'her. del quon. Pacifico Pontio, & Gio. Battista/ Piccaglia compagni. MDCII./ Con licenza de' Superiori./ 30.2 cm. Cia Fornaroli Collection

6 *Egg dance*

[on plate, at top] Has ducunt choreas, qvi bacchanalia vivunt./ M. de Vos invent. Joan Galle excud./ [below at left] 4 line poem in French [at right] 4 line poem in Dutch/ Engraving 8.15×11.8 plain, bound into a copy of: Charles Compan: Dictionnaire de la Danse . . . Paris, Cailleau, 1787. In Memory of August D. Juilliard

7 *An equestrian ballet in Florence*

Figure della Festa A Cavallo, Rappresentata ne Teatro Del Sermo. Gran Duca di Toscana/ il 15, Luglio 1637/ Agnol. Ricci In. Del ballo Felice Ganb.rai Ingre Ste. de.lla be.lla del e F. [at top] Carro D'Amore/ Engraving 12.11×1?, plain. Plate from: Ferdinando Bardi, conte di Vernio: Descrizione delle feste fatte in Firenze per le reali nozze de Serenissimi sposi Ferdina II. gran duca di Toscana, e Vittoria principes d'Vrbino. Fiorenza, per Zanoli Pignoni, 1637. Gift in memory of Philip J. S. Richardson

8 *Scene from* Le Nozze degli Dei

Qvarta Scena di Mare/ Alfo.vs Parig.vs Inu/ S[tefano] D[ella] B[ella] Delt. e F/ Etching 7.14×11.6 plain. Plate from: Le Nozze degli d Favola dell'Ab' Gio. Carlo Coppola rappresent in musica in Firenze nelle reali nozze de Serenis.mi gran duchi di Toschana Ferdinan II. e Vittoria principessa d'Vrbino [Firenze 1637].Cia Fornaroli Collection

9 *Costume for* Le Triomphe de l'Amour

Habit d'Indien du balet du Triomphe de l'amour./ [on plate:] J. Berin del./ [n d] Engraving 10.2×7.6 plain. Purchase Fun

10 *Costume of a sculptor*

Habit de Sculpteur/ se vend sous les Charnie St. Innocent avec privil' du Roy/ Joan. Berin jn. Jacob. le Pautre Sculp./ [n d] Engraving 10.11×7.5 colored. Purchase Fund

Mazurka des Salons.

11 Les Festes de l'Amour et de Bacchus

[at left] Les Festes de l'Amour et de Bacchus, Comedie en Musique/ representée dans le petit Parc de Versailles/ [center] II./ [at right] Festum Cupidinis et Bacchi, Comoedia ad perpetuum vocum/ et tibiarum cantum acta, In Hortis Versallianis./ le Pautre Sculps 1678./ Engraving 10.10×16.7 plain. Cia Fornaroli Collection

12 A dancing master meditates on ballet

Engraved frontispiece to: Gottfried Taubert/ Tantzmeisters zu Leipzig,/ Rechtschaffener Tantzmeister,/ oder grundliche Erklärung/ der Frantzösischen Tantz-Kunst,/ bestehend in drey Büchern/ . . . Leipzig, bey Freidrich Lanckischers Erben. 1717./ 20.2 cm. Cia Fornaroli Collection

13 Dance notation by Feuillet, 1700

Engraved illustration to: Choregraphie/ ou/ l'Art de De'crire/ La Dance,/ par Caracteres, Figures/ et Signes De'monstratifs,/ . . . Par M. Feuillet, Maître de Dance./ A Paris,/ Chez l'Auteur . . ./ Et chez Michel Brunet . . ./ M.DCC./ Avec Privilege du Roy./ 23.8 cm. Lincoln Kirstein Collection

14 Minuet from Rameau's Maître à Danser

Folding plate, engraving 11.12×10.13 inches, opposite p 53 in: Le Maître a danser,/ . . . Par le Sieur Rameau, Maître à danser des Pages/ de Sa Majesté Catholique la Reine d'Espagne./ Nouvelle Edition./ A Paris,/ Chés Jean Villette Fils, rue S. Jacques,/ à Saint Bernard./ M.DCC.XXXIV./ Avec Approbation & Privilege du Roy./ Lincoln Kirstein Collection

15 Marie Camargo

Mlle. Camargo./ [at left:] Fidele aus loix de la Cadence/ Je forme, au gré de l'art, les pas les plus hardis; [at right:] Originale dans ma danse/ Je puis le disputer aux Balons, aux Blondis/. Peint par N. Lancret. gravé par L. Cars./ A Paris chez l'auteur sur le quai de la Feraille a la croix des Perles. Et chez la veüve Chereau rue St. Jacques aux deux pilliers d'Or. Avec Privilege du Roy./ [n d] Engraving 16.4×22 plain. Purchase Fund

16 Costume for Zephyre

Zéphyre./ J.B. Martin Inv. et Sculpt./ [n d] Engraving 8.14×6.14 plain. Cia Fornaroli Collection

17 Spanish peasant costume in a ballet

Danseur Pantomime dans les Ballets de l'Opera Fesant le Pas de Paisan Espagnol./ [n d] Engraving 12.2×8.3 colored. Cia Fornaroli Collection

18 A minuet, from Bickham's treatise, 1738

Engraved illustration to: An Easy/ Introduction/ to/ Dancing:/ or, The/ Movements in the Minuet/ Fully/ Explained./ . . . By George Bickham, Junior./ London:/ Printed for T. Cooper, at the Globe in Paternoster-Row; and sold/ by the Musick-Shops in Town and Country. MDCCXXXVIII./ (Price One Shilling.)/ 24.2 cm. Friends of the Dance Collection

19, 20 Lady and gentleman in a minuet

Plates to: The/ Rudiments/ of/ Genteel Behavior/ by/ F. Nivelon./ 1737./ 28.4 cm. Cia Fornaroli Collection

21 Grown Gentlemen Taught to Dance

Grown Gentlemen Taught to Dance./ Engraved after an Original Picture of Mr. John Collett, in the Possession of Mr. Smith./ Printed for Jno. Smith, No. 35, in Cheapside, & Robt. Sayer, No. 53, in Fleet Street, as the Act directs 20th Augt. 1768./ Engraving 12.5×9.12 plain. Lincoln Kirstein Collection

22 Mlle Auretti

Mademoiselle/ Auretti/ G. Scotin Sculpt./ Published According to Act of Parliament Jany. ye 15th. 1745/6/ Engraving 17.3×13.6 plain [example from the collection of Queen Victoria]. Lincoln Kirstein Collection

23 A dance in Otaheite, 1777

A Dance in Otaheite./ J. Webber del. J. K. Sherwin sc./ [at top right] 28/ Engraving 8.15×14.14 plain. Plate for: James Cook: A Voyage to the Pacific Ocean. London, 1784, II. Lincoln Kirstein Collection

24 May Ball at Versailles

Bal du May donné à Versailles pendant Le Carnaval de L'année 1763, sous les Ordres de/ M. le Duc de Duras Premier Gentil-homme de la chambre du Roi, et ordonnée par M. DeLaferté/ Intendant et Controlleur Général de L'argenterie menus plaisirs et affaires de La Chambre de sa Majesté/ Delin. M.A. Slodtz Sculp. F.N. Martinet/ [n d] Engraving 9.13×15.5 plain. Purchase Fund

25 Jason et Medée (*Baccelli, Vestris, Simonet*)

Jason et Medee [five bars of engraved music] Ballet Tragique./ Published July 3rd. 1782 by John Boydell Engraver in Cheapside London./ Engraving with bistre wash 14.13×18.2. Cia Fornaroli Collection

26 *Auguste Vestris, 1781*

A Stranger at Sparta standing long upon one Leg, said to a Lacedaemonian,/ I do not believe you can do as much: "True (said he) but every Goose can"./ See Plutarch's Laconic Apothegms Vol. I Page 406/ Published 2st. April 1781/ By Torre No. 44 Market Lane./ [on plate, an inscription in Greek conveying the same meaning as the English anecdote] Engraving 6.3×6.3 plain. Friends of the Dance Collection

27 *Giovanna Baccelli*

[on plate] Signora Baccelli./ Painted by T. Gainsborough R.A. London Pubd. According to Act Feby. 5. 1784 by T Jones No 63 Great Portland Street Marylebone. Engraved by John Jones./ Mezzotint 21.1×13.5 plain. Purchase Fund

28 *Marie Madeleine Guimard, Jean Dauberval, and Marie Allard*

attitudes de danse éxecutées a L'Opera/ par le Sr. Doberval et Mlles Guimard et Allard en 1779/ Dessinées et gravées par P. Lelu peintre/ a Paris chez l'Auteur Rue du Faubourg Mont Martre No. 17/ [n d] Etching 7.1×9 plain. Purchase Fund

29 *King's Theatre in the Haymarket*

Opera House./ London. Pub. 1st March 1809, at R Ackermann's Repository of Arts 101 Strand./ Rowlandson & Pugin delt. et sculpt. J. Bluck aquat./ Aquatint 7.12×9.14 colored. Lincoln Kirstein Collection

30 *Duport's symbolic conquest of Vestris*

Frontispiece to: La Danse,/ ou/ Les Dieux de l'Opéra,/ poëme,/ par J. Berchoux./ A Paris,/ chez Giguet et Michaud, Imp.-Libraires,/ rue des Bons-Enfans, No. 34./ M.DCCC.VI./ 15 cm. Lincoln Kirstein Collection

31 *Mademoiselle Parisot*

Mademoiselle Parisot/ London Published as the Act directs March 11 1797 by A W Devis/ Painted by A W Devis/ Engraved by I R Smith Messotint Engraver to his Royal Highness the Prince of Wales/ Mezzotint 23.1×14.2 plain. Friends of the Dance Collection

32 *Scene from a ballet by Viganò, 1812*

Rupi e scoscesi scogli che si estendono sino al mare formando una rada capace di varj grossi vascelli. di fianco si apre/ l'ingresso ad una vasta ed oscura spelonca./ Questa scena fu eseguita pel Ballo tragico L'alunno della giumenta, ossia l'Ippotoo vendicato, composta e diretto dal Sig. Salvatore Viganò per l'I.R. Teatro alla Scala/ La Primavera dell'Anno 1812/ Milano, Antonio Bossi Editore/ A. Sanquirico inv. e dip. Carolina Lose inc./ Etching and aquatint with wash 10.12×14.12. Cia Fornaroli Collection

33 *Pierre Gardel*

Mr. Gardel le Jeune,/ de l'Académie Royale de Musique./ Dutertre pinx. Carrée Sculp./ [n d] Aquatint 5.3×3.7 colored. Cia Fornaroli Collection

34 *Marie Gardel*

Galerie Théâtrale./ 17.me Liv.on No. 66./ Coeuré del. Déposé à la Direction de la Lib.ie Prud'hon Sculpt./ (Académie R.le de Musique.) Mme. Gardel. (Rôle de Psyché)/ Ballet de Psyché./ Ecrit pas Beaublé Imprimé par Langlois/ [n d] stipple engraving 7.8.×5.15 colored. Purchase Fund

35 *A French dancing school*

[no title, n d] Drawing, pen and ink with wash 7.8×11.10 [Drawing for a colored engraving, "Academie et Salle de Danse. Les Graces Parisiennes," which is also in the Dance Collection]. Purchase Fund

36 *Four couples dancing a quadrille*

L'Eté./ Lebas sculpt./ [on plate:] E/. [n d] Engraving 5.4×7.7 colored. [One of a series of four uniform prints, the others being: La Pastourelle. La Poule. A droite sur les Côtés]. Purchase Fund

37 *Ballet positions from Blasis' Treatise, 1820*

Engraved illustration to: Traité Elémentaire, théorique et pratique/ de l'Art de la Danse/ . . . Par Ch. Blasis/ premier danseur./ Milan, 1820./ Chez Joseph Beati et Antoine Tenenti,/ Rue de S. Marguerite (contr. di S. Margherita), No. 1066./ Imprimerie I.I. Destefanis a S. Zeno, N. 534./ 22 cm. Cia Fornaroli Collection

38 *Classical poses from Theleur's* Letters on Dancing

Engraved illustration to: Letters on Dancing,/ Reducing/ This elegant and healthful Exercise/

la promenade.

la passe.

La valse

Pas Bohémien

to/ Easy Scientific Principles./ . . . by E. A. Théleur,/ . . . London:/ . . . Sherwood & Co., . . . / 1831./ 27.2 cm. Cia Fornaroli Collection

39   Amalia Brugnoli, Jean Rozier, 1823

Hr. Rozier und Dlle. Brugnoli/ im Ballett die Fee und der Ritter./ lith. Institut in Wien. I.J./ [n d] Lithograph vignette 6.2×6 colored. Cia Fornaroli Collection. From the George Chaffee Collection

40   Barrymore's Il Naufragio di La Peyrouse

Esterno di una Capanna/ Questa Scena fu eseguita pel Ballo Pantomimo serio Il Naufragio di La Peyrouse, posto sulle scene dell'I.R. Teatro alla Canobbiana, dal Sig. William Barrymore/ L'Autunno dell'anno 1825./ A. Sanquirico inv. e dip. Carolina Lose inc/ aquatint 11.5×14.5 colored. Lincoln Kirstein Collection

41   Spanish bolero

The Boleras Dance./ Rev.d Wm. Bradford del. T. Clark sculp./ [n d] Aquatint vignette 8.4×11.6 colored. Purchase Fund

42   La Sonnambula

Die Nachtwandlerinn/ Pantomimisches Ballet von Scribe und Aumer./ Haupt scene./ Scholler del. Zinke sc./ Gallerie interessanter und drolliger Scenen, 4te Jahrgang. No. 1./ [n d] Engraving 7.2×9.9 colored. Cia Fornaroli Collection

43   Scene from Jocko, the Brazilian Ape

Joko, der brasilianische Affe./ Ballet von Taglioni./ Scene des glücklichen Wiedersehens./ Schoeller del. Zincke sc./ Gallerie drolliger Scenen 17.t Lieferung./ [n d] Engraving 6.15×9.14 colored. Cia Fornaroli Collection

44, 45, 46, 47   The Dancing Lesson, four caricatures by George Cruikshank

44 [on plate:] The 1st Position/ The Dancing Lesson- Pt. 1./ Etch.d by G. Cruik-k Pub.d by Tho.s McLean 26 Haymarket/ Aug.t 1st 1835/ Etching 4.11×6.3 plain
45 [on plate:] The Minuet./ The Dancing Lesson- Pt: 2./G. Crikshank fect- Pub.d by Thos McLean 26 Haymarket./ Aug.t 1st 1835./ Etching 4.12×6.3 plain
46 [on plate:] L'Ete/ The Dancing Lesson. Pt. 3/ G. Crikshank fec.t- Pub.d by Thos McLean 26 Haymarket/ Aug.t 1st 1835./ Etching

4.13×6.5 plain
47 [on plate:] The Sailors Hornpipe/ The Dancing Lesson Pt.4/ G. Cruikshank fect. Pub.d by Thos McLean 26 Haymarket/ Augt. 1st 1835./ Etching 4.12×6.5 plain. Lincoln Kirstein Collection

48   The Waltz

Le Maitre à danser/ Valse à Trois Temps./ 8./ Paris. Goupil et Vibert. boulevt. Montmartre, 15, et rue de Lancry, 7. Paris. T. Mayer, rue de la vieille Monnaie. 22./ London. Published 1st Novber. 1844, by the Anaglyphic Company, 25, Berners St. Oxford St./ Berlin. Verlag von L. Sachse et Cie./ Anais Colin, pinxt. Sorrieu, lith./ [n d] Lithograph 9.10×7.8 colored. Gift in memory of Arthur H. Franks

49   Taglioni and Mazilier in La Sylphide, 1832

Madlle Taglioni, as La Sylphide,/ in the/ Mountain Sylph./ Painted by G. Lepaulle. Lith of E B. & E.C. Kellogg. Hartford Conn./ [n d] Lithograph 10.11×8.13 colored. Purchase Fund

50, 51, 52, 53, 54, 55   Marie Taglioni in La Sylphide as drawn by Alfred E. Chalon in 1845

[Portfolio with title page and six lithographs] La Sylphide./ Souvenir d'Adieu/ de/ Marie Taglioni/ par/ A.E. Chalon R.A./ Artistes Lithographes/ R.J. Lane A.R.A./ Edward Morton,/ J.S. Templeton,/ J.H. Lynch,/ T.H. Maguire,/ Londres. Septr.15, 1845, publié par J. Mitchell Libraire de sa Majesté,/ 33, Old Bond Street./ A Paris chez Goupil et Vibert Boulevard Montmartre, déposé./ imprimé par M & N Hanhart/
50 1./ Proof/ London Published September 8, 1845, by J. Mitchell, publisher to her Majesty, 33, Old Bond St./ A Paris chez Goupil et Vibert, Boulvt. Montmartre./ M & N Hanhart. Lith Imp. [on stone] A. E. Chalon R.A.   R. J. Lane A.R.A./
51 2./ [same text and format as 1] A. E. Chalon R. A.   J.S. Templeton/
52 3./ [same text and format] A.E. Chalon R.A. Edward Morton/
53 4./ [same text and format] A.E. Chalon R.A. J. H. Lynch/
54 5./ [same text and format] A.E. Chalon R.A. T. H. Maguire/
55 6./ [same text and format] A.E. Chalon R.A. R.J. Lane A.R.A./
Six lithographs, each octagonal 15.15×10.12 plain. Cia Fornaroli Collection. From the George Chaffee Collection

Mazurka à l'Opéra.

56   The Celeste-Al Cabinet, *1836*

The Celeste-Al Cabinet./ Dickenson. Butler.
Cass. Jimmy O'Neal. Door Keeper. Celeste.
General Jackson. Kendal. Woodbury. Van
Buren./ . . . Published April 1836 by H. R.
Robinson 48 Cortland St. N.Y./ Entered
accordg. to Act of Congress in the Year 1836
by H. R. Robinson, in the Clerk's Office of the
District Court of the United States of the
Southern District of New York./ Lithograph
10.14×18.12 colored. Cia Fornaroli Collection

57   *Celeste as the Arab Boy*

Celeste./ as the Arab Boy./ A Sketch by William
Drummond/ [n d] Lithograph octagon
14.12×11.2 colored. Lincoln Kirstein Collection

58   *Eugenie LeComte*

Madame LeComte./ Principal Danseuse at the
Theatres Royal Paris, London, St. Petersburgh
&c./ In the Character of the Abbess, in Robert
le Diable./ Entered according to Act of Congress
in the Year 1837 by H. R. Robinson, in the
Clerk's Office of the District Court of the United
States, for the Southern District of New York/
The Prosecuted Picture. [facsimile autograph:]
H. R. Robinson./ Litho.y of H. R. Robinson,
52 Courtlandt St. N. Y./ [on stone:] E.W.C./
Lithograph vignette 11.8×10.3 colored. Cia
Fornaroli Collection. From the George Chaffee
Collection

59   The Three Graces

The Three Graces./ 416./ Lith. and Pub. by
N. Currier 152 Nassau cor. Spruce St. N. Y./
[on stone:] Taglioni. Elssler. Cerito./ [n d]
Lithograph 11.10×8.6 colored. Cia Fornaroli
Collection

60   *Cecilia McBride*

Miss McBride./ Pendleton's Lithography,
Boston./ [n d] Lithograph 11.8×8.2 plain.
Lincoln Kirstein Collection

61   *Paul and Amelie Taglioni in* La Sylphide

Mons. Paul Taglioni. Madame Taglioni./ In the
Characters of La Sylphide & James Reuben, at
the Park-Theatre, New-York, May 22d.. 1839./
Principal Dancers of the Opera House./
[Berlin, London, etc./] Lith. of H. R. Robinson,
52 Courtlandt St. N.Y./ [illegible signature on
stone: N. Sarony ?] Lithograph trimmed to
8.11×13 colored. Purchase Fund

62   *Fanny Elssler in* La Volière

La Volière- Portrait of Mademoiselle F. Elssle[r]
Printed by P. Gauci, 9, North Crescent,
Bedford Square. Drawn on Stone by M. Gau[c]
from a drawing by J. Deffett Francis. [facsimi[le]
signature:] Fanny Elssler/ London, August
1838, Published by Welch & Gwynne,
Printsellers to the Royal Family, 24, St. Jame[s]
Street. à Paris, chez Rittner & Goupil,
Boulivard Montmartre./ Deposé a la directio[n]
Proof/ Lithograph 20.6×13.6 plain. Friends [of]
of the Dance Collection. From the George
Chaffee Collection

63   *Fanny Cerrito in* La Sylphide

Fanny Cerrito/ nel ballo la Silfide di Cortesi,[/]
Al Signor Bartolomeo Merelli che diede
occasione ai Milanesi/ di ammirare sulle scen[e]
del Gran Teatro della Scala/ L'Esimia Artist[a]
l'autore Roberto Focosi D.D.D./ Milano Lit.
Gallina./ [on stone:] Focosi/ [n d] Lithograp[h]
vignette 16.14×12.10 plain. Cia Fornaroli
Collection

64   *Marie Taglioni in* La Gitana, *1841*

Maria Taglioni/ nel ballo La Gitana/ del
coreografo Signor Filippo Taglioni padre del[l']
esimia artista./ Chi vuol veder quanto inamo[r]
e bei/ Danzar quaggiù come si danza in cielo[/]
S'affretti e venga a rimirar costei./ [on stone]
Focosi/ [n d] Lithograph vignette 17×12.7
plain. Cia Fornaroli Collection

65   *Costume for Marie Taglioni in* Herta

Drawing from an album of 26 original design[s]
water color and ink. Pencil title: Costumes/
Théatre/ Acteurs & Danseurs/ de l'Opéra/
[n d] 24.5 cm. [This page has been signed by
Marie Taglioni.] Friends of the Dance Collect[ion]

66   *Fanny Cerrito in* Alma

[no title, n d] Cerrito with Henri Desplaces
(left) and Jules Perrot (right). Unsigned wat[er]
color [probably by R. J. Hamerton] Octagon
13.8×10.12. Purchase Fund. From the Georg[e]
Chaffee Collection

67   *Grisi and Perrot in* Esmeralda

Madelle. Carlotta Grisi, and Monsr. Perrot./ [In]
the very attractive ballet/ La Esmeralda./
Published by T. Mc.Lean, 26 Haymarket.
April. 6th. 1844./ J. Bouvier, del. Litho.
70. St. Martins Lane./ Lithograph 14.12×11.[6]
colored. Cia Fornaroli Collection. From the
George Chaffee Collection

Mazurka des Salons.

68 Adele Dumilâtre as Myrtha in Giselle, 1843

[facsimile signature:] Adele Dumilatre/ as Myrtha./ in the ballet of Giselle./ London Published by T. McLean. 26 Haymarket. April 20 1843./ Bouvier del. Litho. at the General Establishment, 70 St. Martin's Lane./ Hexagonal lithograph 14.10×10.14 plain. Cia Fornaroli Collection

69 Flora Fabbri in The Devil to Pay

[facsimile signature:] Flora Fabbri/ as Mazourka in the Ballet of the/ Devil to Pay./ Paris, Goupil & Vibert, déposé/ Printed by M & N Hanhart./ J.W. Child, delt. London, Published February 10th 1846, by Messrs. Fores, 41, Piccadilly, corner of Sackville Street. J. Brandard, lith./ Lithograph 15.14×10.14 colored. Cia Fornaroli Collection

70 Marietta Baderna, 1846

Marietta Baderna/ Allieva de' Sigri. Conjugi Blasis professori di perfezionamento all' I.R. Academia di Ballo in Milano./ Prima Danzatrice all'I.R. Teatro alla Scala./ la Primavera del 1846./ Alcuni Ammiratori D.D./ Giuliani dis. Lit. Messaggi Cd. del Cappello 4025/ Lithograph 19.1×15.5 in an engraved decorative border 19.10×15.14 plain. Cia Fornaroli Collection

71 Giovannina King

Figaro Num. 3./ Galleria Artistico-Teatrale/ Giovannina King./ Focosi dis. Somariva eseg. Milano, Lit. Brison e Corbetta/ [biographical sketch follows] Milano Tip. Guglielmini/ [n d] Lithograph 9.5×8.2 in an engraved decorated border 15×11.9 plain. Cia Fornaroli Collection

72 Amalia Ferraris

Amalia Ferraris/ Vicenza 1853./ B. Marcovich fect. Vicenza Lit. Longo/ [n d] Lithograph vignette 13.4×6.5 plain. Cia Fornaroli Collection

73 A Neapolitan tarantella

Frontispiece, colored lithograph, to: Tarantella/ Ballo Napolitano/ Disegnato da Gaetano Dura Diretto da Pasquale Chiodi/ A.S.F./ La Siga. Principessa d'Ottajano/ Duchessa di Miranda/ Federico Gatti/ D. D. D./ Litografia Gatti Vico 20: Monte Calvario No. 4./ 1834/ 20.3 cm. Purchase Fund

74 Sofia Fuoco in a tarantella

Sofia Fuoco/ nella/ Tarantella/ Lit. Ach. Paris, Firenze./ [on stone:] Sanesi/ [n d] Lithograph

oval in floral border 11.6×8.13 colored. Cia Fornaroli Collection

75 Pas de Quatre (Taglioni, Grisi, Cerrito, Grahn) 1845

Music cover, trimmed example, title lacking. [Marie Taglioni, Carlotta Grisi, Fanny Cerrito and Lucile Grahn in the Pas de Quatre, by Pugni, 1845. By and after John Brandard] Lithograph 11.1×8.12 colored. Cia Fornaroli Collection

76 Nathalie Fitzjames

Mlle. Nathalie Fitz-James./ Alex Lacauchie. Lith: J. Rigo et Cie./ Paris, Publié par Marchant./ [n d] Lithograph vignette 7.11×5.12 plain. Cia Fornaroli Collection

77 Hermine Blangy in Giselle

[no title, n d] Lithograph vignette 15.3×11.8 partly colored [untitled version of a lithograph by Charles Currier after Francis Davignon and Joseph Vollmering, of Hermine Blangy in Giselle]. Purchase Fund

78 Giovanna Ciocca

Sigra. Ciocca/ nella Andalusa (Park Theatre, New York)/ Drawn by F. Davignon./ [n d] Lithograph octagon 15.9×12.6 in an engraved floral border 18×14.13 colored. Purchase Fund

79 Harvest Dance of the Viennese children

The Harvest Dance/ of the/ Viennoise Children./ Atwill, Publisher, 201 Broadway New York./ Lith. and Printed in Colors by Sarony & Major, 117, Fulton St. N.Y./ [n d] Music cover, lithograph 10×9.1 in a decorative floral border, colored [trimmed example]. Lincoln Kirstein Collection

80 Redowa Polka

Pasquale Borri/ H Frappart Fle. Ricci H Vienna/ Redowa Polka/ Girolamo Franceschini dess. Litografia die C Horegschj/ [n d] Lithograph 10.14×9 including decorative border with a medallion bust portrait of Borri, plain. Cia Fornaroli Collection

81 Polish Dance

Polnischer Tanz./ (Wesele w oycowie)/ Berlin, F. Sala & Co. Unter d. Linden 57. Druck v. H. Waldow jun/ New York Max Jacoby & Zeller/ [n d] Lithograph 10.10×15.5 colored. Purchase Fund

Mazurka des Salons

Mazurka Nationale

82   *Tarantella in* L'Étoile de Messine, *1861*

Musée de Moeurs en Actions/ Scène de l'Opéra
La Tarantelle. (Étoile de Messine.)/ Peint par
Morlon Imp. Lemercier, 57, R. de Seine, Paris.
Lith. par Regnier, Bettanier, Morlon/ 8./ Paris,
Eugène Jouy, 56, Boulev'd de Sébastopol.
New-York, Emile Seitz, 413 Broadway/ [n d]
Lithograph 15.8×20.12 colored. Purchase Fund

83   *The Ronzani Ballet*

Ronzani's Grand Ballet Troupe/ from the
Theatre La Scala in Milan the Royal Theatre in
Turin, Her Majesty's Theatre London, Academy
of Music Philadelphia/ lith. by B. F. Smith. Jr.
N.Y. Printed in tints, by F. Michelin. 169
Broadway. N.Y./ [n d] Lithograph 18.15×25.11
colored. Cia Fornaroli Collection. From the
George Chaffee Collection

Page 1   Fritellino

Engraved illustration to: Bernard Picart:
Titulus Stultorum. [Amsterdam, 1696.
Manuscript title: Commedia dell'Arte/ 12
Figures./ 1720. C del A./ 15/] 19.6 cm. From
the library of Gordon Craig

Pages 80–86   *Vignettes from*

La Polka./ Paris (Mon Aumont) François
Delarue Succ. rue J.J. Rousseau, 10 Imp.
Lemercier. London, pub. 20 October by the
Anaglyphic Company, 25 Berners St. Oxford
St./ [9 vignettes titled: La promenade, La valse,
La valse roulée, Pas Bohémien, La poursuite,
Le dos à dos, Le moulinet, Pas Bohémien en
valsant, La passe. n d] Lithograph 15.11×13.4
colored. Purchase Fund

and

La Mazurka./ Paris (Mon Aumont) François
Delarue Succ, rue J.J. Rousseau, 10. Imp.
Lemercier. London- pub. 10 November by the
Anaglyphic Company, 25 Berners St. Oxford
St./ [3 vignettes titled: Mazurka à l'Opéra,
3 titled: Mazurka des Salons, 3 titled: Mazurka
Nationale. n d] Lithograph 15.12×13.4 colored.
Purchase Fund

Cover paper motifs adapted from

Le Rigaudon de la paix (plates 4–7) engraved
illustrations to: Choregraphie/ ou/ l'Art de
De'crire/ La Dance,/ par Caracteres, Figures/
et Signes De'monstratifs,/ . . . Par M. Feuillet,
Maître de Dance./ A Paris,/ Chez l'Auteur . . ./
Et chez Michel Brunet . . ./ M.DCC./ Avec
Privilege du Roy./ 23.8 cm. Lincoln Kirstein
Collection

Mazurka à l'Opéra

Mazurka à l'Opéra.

la valse roulée

This Book, designed by Bert Waggott, was set in Monotype and foundry Bulmer by The Stinehour Press, Lunenburg, Vermont. Offset printing was done by The Meriden Gravure Company, Meriden, Connecticut, on Mohawk Superfine Text supplied by Lindenmeyr Schlosser Paper Company. Binding was done by Russell-Rutter Company, Inc., New York.